CHARLES DARWIN

POCKET
GIANTS

CHARLES DARWIN

POCKET
GIANTS

STEPHEN
WEBSTER

The
History
Press

Acknowledgements

Thanks are due to Tony Morris for his constant encouragement. Richard Milner has for many years provided me with wise and humorous insights into nineteenth-century biology and was helpful with the manuscript. Luca Webster applied the unique scrutiny of an 11-year-old to the task of checking the references, while the rest of my family showed a level of patience worthy of Darwin himself.

Cover image © Mary Evans Picture Library

First published 2014

The History Press
The Mill, Brimscombe Port
Stroud, Gloucestershire, GL5 2QG
www.thehistorypress.co.uk

© Stephen Webster, 2014

British Library Cataloguing in Publication Data.
A catalogue record for this book is available from the British Library.

ISBN 978 0 7524 9940 6

Typesetting and origination by The History Press
Printed in Malta by Gutenberg Press Ltd.

Contents

1

Giant

I think that I am superior to the common run of men in noticing things which easily escape attention, and in observing them carefully. My industry has been nearly as great as it could have been in the observation and collection of facts. What is far more important, my love of natural science has been steady and ardent.

Charles Darwin[1]

Science looks forward: it anticipates rather than remembers. As a result, while the scientific future catches our imagination for its remarkable challenges and potential solutions, the scientific past becomes a hazy landscape, monochrome and flat, and almost never looked at by those who work in a laboratory.

Darwin is different. Darwin's name has never faded. When he died in 1882 he was the most celebrated scientist of his day, and he remains a vivid figure whose work still shapes biology and influences the way we know ourselves. His life was a combination of early adventure, of 'seeing everything', followed by years of contemplation on his favourite scientific problem: the formation of new species. He pursued his ideas with remarkable insight and diligence; Darwin is a giant not simply for the significance of his ideas, but also for the personal qualities he brought to science.

What marks out Darwin's imagination? For him there was no 'flash of genius'. He liked to work slowly and methodically on a range of particular but varied scientific problems – as various as the origin of coral reefs and the behaviour of bees. A cautious man, he built up intellectual credit over many years, which in turn sustained him as he carefully, almost secretly, moved towards a solution to the problem that preoccupied him above all others.

Darwin had an interesting mix of qualities. He was sensitive to others' feelings, yet candid about what he thought of people. He was fearful of causing controversy, yet spent a life drawing up one of science's most radical theories. He could be lively and sociable, but also reclusive and depressed. It was his great good fortune to be wealthy enough to live as a country squire, enjoying family and work for more than forty years in his rural fastness, Down House. He could pull on his boots and be tramping through the countryside in an instant, a valuable counterpoint to the intensiveness of the study where he wrote his books. His imagination depended on those walks, but he was near enough to London for scientific friends to visit him for enjoyably talkative dinners and weekends. He was prodigiously creative and hard-working, while also hampered by illness for long periods.

Darwin was far from the conventional image of a stern Victorian patriarch. He was a perceptive and loving father: he had ten children, and seven survived childhood. The illnesses that struck his family with fatal effect were devastating to him. More usually, as the children crashed around the house, Darwin absorbed their lively spirit and was a playmate. He never saw himself as impressively academic, and his formal education had a discernible limp. Yet he was always interested in nature and from the beginning flavoured his schooling with his own studies of science. By his late teens, he had expertise in botany, zoology and geology, a serious training in natural history which for years ran alongside his studies of the classics, medicine and divinity.

It was his own programme of learning, not his university degree, that got him a place on the scientific survey ship HMS *Beagle* for a five-year round-the-world trip. Once aboard, his relaxed and secure temperament helped him thrive in those cramped and stringent ocean-going conditions. He even managed to get on well with Captain FitzRoy, one of the Royal Navy's most difficult and intransigent characters.

The *Beagle* voyage lasted five years, taking him to South America, Australia and all points between. Those years, 1831 to 1836, were the making of Darwin: a raw mix of adventure, physical challenge and exciting intellectual and emotional discovery. It was on the *Beagle* that he first began to ask about the origin of species, questions that set him on his lifetime's path. And his account of this time, *The Beagle Diary*, is one of the great descriptions of travel – and of youthful endeavour.

Darwin made a name for himself during that trip. People he admired noticed his astute scientific commentaries, which he posted back to England during the voyage. When he eventually returned to London, and began to sort and describe his specimens, he could activate a ready-made network of scientists, roping them in for their expert opinions and for their patronage. Over and above all this, he came home with his own big idea: a vast project in mind, a more-or-less secret urge to explain how life on Earth had changed over time.

Darwin was a pioneer biologist but he didn't work alone. Fourteen thousand letters exist in the archives, and are available online. There is much documentation besides this correspondence. A collector from a young age, he was always meticulous in his record keeping – his household accounts are preserved, for example, as are his books, with all their revealing marginalia. The archive of 'Darwiniana' is vast. It is the reason we know so much about the way he lived and worked. And it is an archive which proves that science cannot be split from personality, or from society.

Darwin groaned when he wrote his books, and there are vivid descriptions of his toils. But on the *Beagle* voyage, with so many ideas pressing in, writing became an important part of his life. He could not draw well and photography did not exist yet. FitzRoy and Darwin discussed their ideas about science, but their conversations were sometimes fraught, for it turned out that Captain FitzRoy's political views included a tolerance of slavery, a practice Darwin and his parents had always abhorred. He took to writing down his ideas, and his intellectual development can be traced in the filling of notebook after notebook, the compilation of his great journal and in letters that might take days to write and six months to reach home. The climax of this endeavour was his book *On the Origin of* Species (known here simply as *The Origin*), published suddenly in 1859 after two decades of gestation and hesitation. Already a renowned scientist before the book was issued, *The Origin* was of such wide interest to society that Darwin quite quickly became world famous.

What was the significance of *The Origin*?

First, it launched biology as a modern science. Before it, there was no agreed-upon explanation for how new species were formed. Darwin changed that. He showed how something admittedly marvellous and enchanting – the way organisms fit their environment so beautifully – needs no supernatural creator, but can be explained by ordinary biological processes.

Second, *The Origin* put human beings into the frame of nature. No longer were people self-evidently separate from the natural world; the suggestion now was that they had emerged from that world through evolution and still bore its imprint. When Darwin published his great work in 1859 he was not confident enough to talk about human evolution, so he put his energy into arguing that modern species descended from ancient ones we see in the fossil record. That, he felt, was ambitious enough: the transmutation of species (the word 'evolution' gained its modern meaning later in the nineteenth century) was a highly controversial concept. He could not, however, resist making a brief comment right at the end of his book: 'Light will be thrown on the origin of man and his history.'[2] No one could miss the point. Darwin argued with unassailable precision and steadfastness that modern organisms are similar to extinct forms in the fossil record because one was descended from the other. He called it 'descent with modification'; we all know it as evolution. If this was convincing for plants and animals – and Darwin took twenty-three years to make sure he got it right – it was hard to see why humans should be any different.

Third, *The Origin* launched ecology and ecological awareness. It is said that when, in 1968, the *Apollo* astronauts took a photograph of the Earth from space – a floating blue orb in a pitch-dark surround – the idea of nature as a whole became suddenly obvious. But *The Origin* made the point with equal clarity over a century earlier. It has an emphatic message: we all are linked together, and we all are linked to our environment. Darwin provided the intellectual roots for environmentalism.

Darwin is a giant because he provided science with one of its most powerful theories, and provoked humanity into new ways of thinking about itself and about planet Earth. In the years since his death, biology has been elaborating and adding to his scientific insights, and humans have begun to come to a sense of the importance of their stewardship of the planet. No single scientist has done more to remind us of our animal origins or of our moral responsibility towards the Earth we inhabit.

2

Early Years

I have heard my father and elder sisters say that I had, as a very young boy, a strong taste for long solitary walks, but what I thought about I know not ... I was very fond of collecting eggs, but I never took more than a single egg out of a bird's nest.

Charles Darwin[3]

Darwin was born into a thriving family. Around him were lively siblings, a father with a good income and a mother whose own family, the Wedgwoods, were busily growing their pottery industry in the north Midlands of England. Charles' paternal grandfather Erasmus was a physician and a famous poet, one smitten by the progressive aspects of technology. Evolutionary theory clearly ran in the family, for the great poet had believed that species transformed over time. He had described a theory of evolution in his *Zoonomia*, published in 1794.[4]

It was Erasmus Darwin who had first forged the family link with the Wedgwoods, joining them in their campaigns to get London politicians to work harder for the industrial north – 'England's powerhouse'. The Wedgwoods were wealth creators, suspicious of the parliamentary powers of the English aristocracy, but their political interests were wide. They were convinced of the wrongness of slavery and were restless believers in the power of science and technology to improve the wealth of the nation and the happiness of its citizens. The shared Darwin–Wedgwood passion for technology and politics became a bloodline when the Wedgwood daughter, Susannah, married the Darwin son, Robert.

It perhaps isn't a surprise, then, that their fourth child, Charles, always maintained a keen interest in the currents of political thought.

Darwin grew up in an atmosphere of progressive politics and optimism about the value of technology. A key part of this influence was the Wedgwood allegiance to the Unitarian Church. As Nonconformist Christians worshipping outside the Church of England, they were by definition dissident thinkers, convinced of the promise of science and reason, and inclined to question the powers of the political and religious establishment. A link between scientific work and religious belief had been established by the founder of modern Unitarianism, the eighteenth-century chemist Joseph Priestley, who worked with the Wedgwoods and was a friend of Erasmus Darwin. A pragmatic collaboration between religion and science formed the background to Darwin's upbringing and it meant that when he started thinking about the evolution of species, he was in tune with a free-thinking tradition already existing in his family.

Among the Unitarian doctrines Darwin absorbed as a child was a belief in the essential unity of all people. He lived in a household that saw humankind as indivisible and slavery a horror that must be campaigned against. Even if he was not directly involved in those campaigns, his mother had been. The Wedgwoods' tough-minded idealism must be a factor not only in Darwin's lifelong abhorrence of slavery, but also in his willingness to fight for his beliefs, however fierce the opposition.

The family house was a large mansion on the edge of Shrewsbury, close to meadows that Darwin was soon exploring. Built by Robert to mark his success as a doctor and family man, the Mount, as it was called, was his 'seat', and he was its undoubted patriarch. When Charles once described his father as 'the largest man I ever knew',[5] he meant it literally as well as metaphorically, for Robert was indeed vast, weighing in at some 24 stone (336 pounds). But he was a big character, too, a respected physician who was attentive to his patients and good at his job.

The remarkable doctor had other professional interests. At a time when commerce and industry were expanding fast across rural England, he formed a kind of personal bank, loaning to individuals as they tried to grow their land or their businesses. It was something he was good at and wanted to do, for he respected these energetic innovators. He knew his clients well enough to intuit when to lend and when to decline. According to Darwin, his father's 'chief mental characteristics were his power of observation and his sympathy, neither of which have I ever seen exceeded or even equalled'.[6] By the time Darwin was a teenager, the doctor was managing two successful practices, one in medicine, the other in banking. Both skills secured his importance and reputation across the county – and made the family rich.

Darwin kept his father in mind always. There is a story of Charles visiting the Mount as an old man, and being shown round by the new tenant, regretting all the while that the visit was so closely supervised: 'If I could have been left alone in that green house for five minutes, I know I should have been able to see my father in his wheel-chair as vividly as if he had been there before me.'[7] When the time came for Darwin's own children to describe their memories of a notable father, they remembered how he was forever reminding them of their excellent grandfather – 'the wisest man I ever knew'.[8]

Darwin's appreciation of his father is understandable. For beyond the helpful matter of Robert's financial success, it seems his undisputed power in all family matters was combined with some sensitivity to Darwin's ambling development. Robert was a shrewd man who acted decisively and presciently at critical moments in his son's student years. Darwin's false starts and waywardness never produced a family panic, and he became in due course a young man of determination and courage, well able to stand up for himself and with a firm sense of his true vocation.

Darwin had four sisters and one brother. Ras (full name Erasmus) was four years his senior, but the gap didn't seem to matter. They were fellow conspirators as teenagers and college companions later. They stayed fond of each other throughout their lives and it is significant that Ras is buried in the village churchyard at Downe, where Darwin settled and spent most of his adulthood. Ras never married – his sisters described him as too lazy for that – but he was a genial conversationalist, dryly humorous and much too worried about his health.

Darwin was the youngest boy, but not the youngest child. Chivvying from behind was Catherine, just fourteen months his junior. Catherine also was a friend. An attractive engraving exists of these two smallest additions to the family. Catherine and Darwin gaze out of the frame; they look good natured and happy, as though poised for a life made easier by privilege and doting siblings. Their mother, Susannah Wedgwood, and three older sisters formed the sturdy domestic backbone of the family.

Tragically, that backbone weakened over time. When Charles was 8 years old his mother died, hit by an infection that raced rapidly and painfully through her system. The doctor could do nothing. Aunts and sisters attended what fast became a deathbed. Charles was kept away. His Aunt Kitty reported back to the Wedgwoods: 'After a wretched night my poor sister yet lives, but the mortification is far advanced and must very soon be fatal.'[9] Susannah endured this catastrophic illness – probably pleurisy – for three days before dying. It was an exhausting and pitiable end, and Charles was to see her only when she was relaxed once more in death. This shocking and disastrous event left him with only the faintest of memories, and years later he made this sad comment about her: 'My mother died in July 1817 when I was a little over eight years old, and it is odd that I can remember hardly anything about her except her deathbed, her black velvet gown, and her curiously constructed work-table.'[10] The elder sisters, who from the beginning had doted on their little brother, were now in charge of the household and of their young siblings. Marianne, Caroline and Susan were 19, 17 and 14 respectively. They knew what to do.

Meanwhile, young Darwin developed a liking for collecting, albeit with no great focus: stones, insects and stamps would all equally catch his eye. It was a fresh-air childhood, and there were aspects of it that he never relinquished. The greater part of his life was spent away from any city, and the childhood passion for collecting grew as he did, pushing aside more formal education and leading in time to his systematic study of great swathes of the natural world. The greatness of Darwin has much to do his with his ability, when young, to maintain a polite interest in his studies, while at the same time allowing his true interests to flourish.

However much Darwin enjoyed his freedom in the countryside, there was no avoiding the schoolmaster and the textbook. Soon after Susannah's death the family decided it was time to get a grip on the boy's schooling. The family was familiar with Shrewsbury School, a famous boarding establishment close by. Ras was already there. It was natural that his younger brother would follow, and a year after his mother's death the 9-year-old Darwin was uprooted from the Mount. Always modest about his formal academic abilities, Darwin looked back at his time at Shrewsbury School with disappointment: 'Nothing could have been worse for the development of my mind than Dr Butler's school, as it was strictly classical, nothing else being taught, except a little ancient geography and history. The school as a means of education to me was simply a blank.'[11]

Yet there were warm memories too. He found a good spot – a deep window in some old wall – where he spent hours reading: Shakespeare for his stories, Euclid for his geometrical clarity. These authors, too, were windows into nature. Nor does it sound as though he was sullen or lonely at Shrewsbury: 'I had many friends amongst the schoolboys, whom I loved dearly, and I think that my disposition was then very affectionate.'[12]

Shrewsbury School, he said, allowed him to be 'a true schoolboy'. Perhaps those great blank spaces of time, familiar to all who have been to boarding school, suited him. In any case, he could always liven things up simply by running away. Home was barely a mile away. Between evening roll call and 'lock up' there was time enough to race over to the Mount, an illicit pleasure that excited his sisters and made his father frown. The sprint back to school before the locks turned 'was generally successful – but when in doubt I prayed earnestly to God to help me, and I well remember that I attributed my success to the prayers and not to my quick running, and marvelled how generally I was aided'.[13]

There were other pleasures too. Ras was a senior at the school and had been hit by a craze for chemistry. The brothers agreed they needed to build a small hut in the garden – a place to do their experiments. It was their own secret world, growing under the benevolent eye of the doctor, an enclave of science a little separate from the Mount. The enthusiasm and the experimenting carried on even when Ras went up to Cambridge to begin his university studies. Letters to his younger brother suggested designs for shelving and various essential devices: 'I got a very nice little blow pipe made of glass for one shilling and sixpence, which gives a great deal of heat ...'[14] Ras was almost beside himself with excitement about equipment – he had come across exactly the right shop in Cambridge: 'It quite made my mouth water to see all the jars and stopcocks and all sorts of things, graduated tubes, blow pipes, cubic inch measures, test tubes, and ye Lord knows what besides.'[15]

Even with Ras at university, the two brothers kept in close touch. The elder brother was reassuring: 'I think my *vacation* and your *holidays* will about fit ...'[16] 'I have just been to chapel, in which respect we are better off than you, as we are only obliged to attend seven days a week.'[17] The brothers continued their immersion in chemical elements and compounds, Ras supervising by post. Charles was laboratory assistant, twisting Dr Darwin's arm from time to time for the necessary cash to fund the experiments.

With Ras an inspiration, Charles was getting on with his own style of education. His later interests – and skills – as an experimental biologist must stem from this time. The trouble was that the more conventional schooling at Shrewsbury was coming off second best. It was obvious Charles was not thriving on Headmaster Butler's curriculum. He wasn't good at the classics and he wasn't good at maths. On the other hand, he was a popular boy, and he certainly wasn't lethargic.

The doctor clearly found Charles to be good company. Together they would wander around the garden at the Mount, looking at the plants. Robert Darwin's brothers were dead, and his own childhood, under the haphazard stewardship of the energetic Erasmus, had been fraught. He found it reassuring to see the two brothers plotting chemistry experiments in their garden lab. Despite the death of his wife, the family was holding together. Looking at Ras and Charles collaborating on experiments, Robert decided that theirs was a relationship worth nurturing. Charles had reached 16. Might there be some way to get the two of them studying together at the same institution? Ras was due to leave Cambridge and move on to a medical school. Why not put Charles down for medicine too, and send them both to Edinburgh? He would be too young to enrol formally, but there would be no problem slipping him in by the back door. Edinburgh was family territory: Grandfather Erasmus had studied there, as had Robert. He had plenty of contacts in the Scottish capital. And so it was decided: aged 16, Charles left Shrewsbury School, returned to the Mount and prepared for life as a university student.

3

Student Lives

Cambridge, I find, is one of the few places, where if you anticipate a great deal of pleasure you do not find yourself disappointed ... in the evenings I generally go out somewhere, and occasionally dinner parties, where good eating and good talking make a most harmonious whole.

Charles Darwin, letter to Caroline Darwin,
28 April 1831[18]

For Darwin, Edinburgh was a fresh life. He knew next to nothing of city ways: Shrewsbury was a market town of shopkeepers and farmers, Edinburgh a city famous for its philosophers and architecture. Here in front of him was the spectacular looming castle on its volcanic rock, the elegant main thoroughfare of Princes Street and the geometric town planning of the Georgian 'New Town'. Down beyond the docks of Leith lay the estuary of the River Forth, with its mudflats and beaches – a dramatic contrast to the soft English meadows of Shropshire.

Best of all, he was reunited with Ras, students together. Excitedly the brothers sent word to the Mount. They had found lodgings: 'Our landlady, by name Mrs Mackay, is a nice clean old body.' The doctor duly learnt about 'very nice and *light* bedrooms and a nice sitting room'.[19] Charles' letter ended by mentioning that he and Erasmus had that very morning been to church – and had been surprised to find the sermon lasted only twenty minutes. The boys were clearly enjoying themselves.

Their sisters sent encouraging letters. Even the youngest of the family, Catherine, joined in, teasing Charles about his spelling: 'I must just mention that Edinburgh is spelt with an *h* at the end; and *altogether* has only one *l*.'[20] She told Charles how much she, and the dog Spark, had been missing him, but also assured him that she was trying to keep her life at home as interesting as his no doubt was becoming: 'I have not told you how gay we have been lately; we have been as constant play goers as you can have been.'[21]

Charles had enjoyed doing doctor's rounds at home in Shrewsbury, under the gaze of his perceptive father. The Edinburgh medical experience was a stark contrast. Years later he recalled it all too clearly: 'The instruction at Edinburgh was altogether by lectures, and these were intolerably dull ... there are no advantages and many disadvantages in lectures compared with reading. Dr Duncan's lectures on *Materia Medica* at 8 o'clock on a winter's morning are something fearful to remember.'[22]

Whatever the miseries of the teaching, however, at least Ras and Charles could suffer together: favourite books, long walks and jokes about the lecturers kept them going. Sensing trouble, the sisters kept up the pressure from home: 'Caroline sends you her love and thanks for your nice and agreeable letter. – Your description of the Lecturers is not very promising, but I hope Dr Duncan will continue to improve.'[23] The doctor didn't write himself, but Charles' sisters passed on his messages: don't be picky about lectures as you cannot really know which ones will prove useful; it was just a fact of life that there would be 'stupid and dry work'.[24]

In his second year the screw turned. Erasmus left to finish his studies in London; Charles was on his own, suddenly bereft in the Scottish metropolis. His medical studies began to falter. In that first year at Edinburgh the boys had been able to groan together and console themselves with each other's company. Now he had no elder brother to follow and laugh with, and no obvious friends. Letters could go back and forth to Shrewsbury, but there could be no running home 'before lock-up'. Still only 17, Charles' disaffection with his medical studies was turning into an intolerable burden.

Characteristically, he found his escape in nature. In the first year, after gloomy medical lectures, the brothers' nature walks out of Edinburgh had been a delight and a relief. Charles decided he would carry on, with or without Ras, helping himself, as greedily as possible, to the delights of Scottish natural history. Of course, the medical studies must continue. But now Charles had something to occupy him properly. He would indulge his favourite pastime and make sure his timetable allowed for plenty of rambling in the countryside. He would also become systematic about learning geology and natural history from some of the resident wise men of Edinburgh.

Charles' freelance studies gathered pace. Edinburgh operated a kind of educational open market. A medical student would sign up for certain courses in order to pursue a medical training and follow the basic medical curriculum. But there were plenty of additional science courses, too, on geology, botany, zoology and astronomy. It was just a matter of registering and paying up. After his immersion in classics at Shrewsbury, and the formidable professional focus of Edinburgh medical studies, here at last was freedom. Natural history could become the organising principle of his life. A critical point in Darwin's intellectual and emotional development had been reached.

Charles signed up for a natural history course and joined a student scientific society, the Plinian. Now he could learn about things that interested him, especially geology, and discuss them at meetings with like-minded enthusiasts. This was how he fell in with Robert Grant, a young lecturer in zoology who had spent time in Paris. Grant was an atheist and, just as daring, believed that species were not fixed, but changed over time. Grant and Charles went down to Leith, where the teacher taught the student important skills in collecting, identifying and dissecting. Charles had been a dry-land collector in Shropshire. Here in Edinburgh he began sampling marine invertebrates. He lifted rocks, sifted mud and filled buckets with pulsing molluscs and crustacea, lugging them back to university to be examined under the microscope. Grant was disciplined and dogged; studying the wildlife of the Firth of Forth was physically challenging, especially in a Scottish winter. The technical skills Darwin garnered were hard won but invaluable.

Unfortunately, outings to the Forth were no compensation for the tedium of studying medicine. Life for Darwin was becoming an unbearable toil. 'Dr Duncan is so very learned that his wisdom has left no room for his sense,' he wrote to Caroline.[25] And after the domestic pleasures of Dr Darwin's pastoral countryside visits, the practical reality of early nineteenth-century treatment was simply horrific.

Early on in his studies Charles saw a child under the knife – before the 'blessed days of chloroform', as he put it.[26] He rushed away before the operation was complete.

In the end, the doctor saw that Charles had stalled and began to think through some possible solutions. On the positive side, his son had plenty of energy – that much was plain from the holiday periods, when Charles pursued with vigour his twin passions for shooting and natural history. But medicine clearly had not inspired him. Robert was not inclined to force Charles along the wrong road: he knew what that was like, for grandfather Erasmus had been domineering and controlling in Robert's early career. Another solution would have to be found.

The basic situation was clear to both father and son. There was enough money in the family to obviate any need to find an income. But Charles had to do something of value and repute. There could be no compromise on that, especially now that he was getting older. As he put it, his father 'was very properly vehement against my turning [into] an idle sporting man, which then seemed my probable destination'.[27] Dr Darwin suggested to Charles that a career in the Church might be the way forward.

Charles wasn't pious, and he wasn't much interested in Church affairs. Thinking back on it later, he wrote, 'Considering how fiercely I have been attacked by the orthodox, it seems ludicrous that I once intended to become a clergyman.'[28] The plan being mapped out was, nonetheless, a good one. Surely with his connections, a good parish could be found, one in the countryside with nature on hand – somewhere he could write his sermons, fetch his butterfly net and head for the outdoors.

Some homework was necessary. Charles' school knowledge of Latin and Greek had evaporated by now, so he crammed the ancients to prepare him for university entrance. He arrived in Cambridge in January 1828, nine months after saying goodbye to Edinburgh and his medical career. Life could begin again.

Charles' three years at Christ's College, Cambridge were far more enjoyable than the alienating medical nightmare he had endured in Edinburgh – much more to his taste. It turned out that a congenial second cousin, William Fox, was also at the university, and likewise aiming to become a clergyman after graduation. Crucially, Fox was keen on natural history; indeed, he was rather expert. Like Charles, he enjoyed shooting and riding. The two became fast friends and together explored the Cambridge surroundings in search of Fox's special interest: beetles. When separated by the first summer break, Charles complained, 'I am dying by inches, from not having any body to talk to about insects.'[29]

With Fox on hand to discuss both the classics and the *Insecta*, Charles could better balance his studies and his obsession with natural history. Cambridge made only faint demands on Charles' time and there was no question of him suffering from his studies as he had in Edinburgh. He was older, too, and the social scene at Cambridge suited him better. He could study in the morning and ride out into the countryside in the afternoon (he had a horse of his own at Cambridge) before dining in hall. Nor was his passion for beetles – he was developing a reputation by now – the cause of any sort of social awkwardness or embarrassment, for the proper celebration of the wonders of nature, perhaps by way of a small private collection, was a common Victorian pastime. For clergymen a decent knowledge of natural history could happily bump alongside an interest in Holy Scripture.

Thinking back on his Cambridge years, Charles once again describes himself as quite unsuited to formal education:

> My time was sadly wasted there, and worse than wasted. From my passion for shooting and for hunting, and, when this failed, for riding across country, I got into a sporting set, including some dissipated low-minded young men ... we sometimes drank too much, with jolly singing and playing at cards afterwards. I know that I ought to feel ashamed of days and evenings thus spent, but as some of my friends were very pleasant, and we were all in the highest spirits, I cannot help looking back to these times with much pleasure.[30]

All this happiness was fruitful, of course: he did perfectly well in his university exams, graduating successfully in 1831.

It was a Cambridge scientist, Rev. John Henslow, who finally managed to help integrate the young Darwin's technical skills in natural history with his restless desire to learn more. Ras had already alerted Charles to Henslow's virtues: his botany lectures were excellent and he was good company, too. Not only was he 'a man who knew every branch of science, and I was accordingly prepared to reverence him',[31] but he was also – Darwin emphasised the point in his later autobiography – a man of immense virtue and moral courage. He had no vanity, was measured in temper and had the most 'winning and courteous manners'. Moreover, he was an interesting teacher and organised good field trips to the fens. Charles, always a fine judge of genuine expertise, was hooked, and duly fell in with Henslow. Where Grant had been his mentor in Edinburgh, Henslow now took on that role in Cambridge.

Henslow put his mind to the question of his student's further training. What was needed was an imaginative approach to Charles' informal education in natural history. He suggested that perhaps they should travel to Tenerife, with its volcanic formations and tropical climate. Some preparation would be needed and when word came that a colleague of Henslow's, Adam Sedgwick, was about to set off on a geological survey of Wales, Darwin was lined up as an assistant. It was a tough, demanding experience, for 'Sedgwick often sent me on a line parallel to his … I have little doubt he did this for my good, as I was too ignorant to have aided him'.[32] The trip was a success, and Charles returned to Shrewsbury a functioning geologist. He was ready now for the trip to Tenerife – and ready too for the shooting season. But on arriving late one night at his family home, Darwin found a letter from Henslow, containing news that would change his life forever.

4

World Traveller

The Voyage is to last 2 years and if you take plenty of books with you, anything you please may be done ... In short I suppose there never was a finer opportunity for a man of zeal and spirit ... I think you are the very man they are in search of.

J.S. Henslow, letter to Charles Darwin,
24 August 1831[33]

Charles was 22 and held in his hand a letter that promised a revolution in his life. After the false start of Edinburgh, the training at Cambridge had run according to plan; just ahead lay the life of the rural clergyman. Charles knew that a country parsonage would soon be his, a comfortable seat where he could combine the duties of work with his passion for natural history. For years he had been weaving together the two strands of his life. He now had the humanities degree he needed for entering the priesthood, plus a growing scientific reputation among people he admired. His father and sisters could all see that the young man's life was coming together well. The last thing the Darwin family needed was a seductive letter from a Cambridge mentor promising their just-settled Charles the journey of a lifetime.

Henslow's letter was prompted by an unusual problem in need of an unusual solution. The Hydrographer's Office – the scientific arm of the Admiralty – was looking for a 'gentleman-naturalist' to provide company for a talented but mercurial naval captain about to set sail for South America as commander of the scientific survey ship HMS *Beagle*. Captain Robert FitzRoy was just 26 and, like Darwin, passionate about his work. But there was a crucial difference between the two men: while Darwin was reliably good-natured, FitzRoy could be irascible and obsessive. The captain himself had put forward the idea that he really ought to have some stabilising company on what promised to be a demanding voyage. In this he was being prudent. The previous captain of the *Beagle*, Pringle Stokes, had shot himself during the ship's first voyage to the Tierra del Fuego; the suicide had created the vacancy that gave FitzRoy his first command. FitzRoy was also concerned about the mental stability of his family. His eminent uncle, Lord Castlereagh, who had run British foreign policy for a decade, had buckled under pressure and cut his throat in 1822.

Captain FitzRoy, well educated in science and maths, was looking for a man of the right class as well as temperament; someone who could converse about interesting scientific matters at his dinner table. The 'companion' would not be an official naturalist – the *Beagle* already had one of those – but it was clear from the start that the chosen person would be free to do as much science as he wished. Hearing all this, Henslow reflected that his lively young friend and protégé Charles Darwin would be a perfect choice.

Summarising the excitement, Henslow was persuasive. 'In short I suppose there never was a finer chance for a man of zeal and spirit,' he wrote.[34] But this was no salaried position: Charles, or rather his father, would have to pay his way. The doctor's moral and financial support was therefore fundamental. Unfortunately, his father did not share Charles' enthusiasm. The ship was likely to be unsafe, he thought, or at the very least uncomfortable.

He considered the adventure yet another interruption to Charles' career, and a disreputable one at that. Moreover, he wondered whether the trip would be of any value at all. No, he could not sanction the madcap scheme. Nor was he likely to change his mind, for the doctor was notorious for his firm and settled views. Charles sent Henslow his thanks and declined the offer. He had never felt more upset. His father had blocked his way and defiance was not an option.

Yet the worldly Robert Darwin had not turned completely against the *Beagle* opportunity. An experienced, successful man, he realised that powerful forces lay behind Henslow's remarkable letter. It was flattering and thought-provoking that Charles had been singled out by the well-respected Cambridge don. And so, on the same day that Darwin wrote to Henslow declining the offer, Robert wrote to his friend Josiah Wedgwood at Maer Hall, where Charles was due for the start of the shooting season. He explained how Charles:

> … will tell you of the offer he has had made to him of going for a voyage of discovery for two years – I strongly object to it on various grounds, but I will not detail my reasons that he may have your unbiased opinion on the subject, and if you think differently from me I shall wish him to follow your advice.[35]

The scene was set for one of the most decisive moments in Darwin's life. He was in Uncle Jos' house, and the place was alive with the news of the nephew's dilemma. Jos, pondering Charles' character, and the nature of the opportunity, made

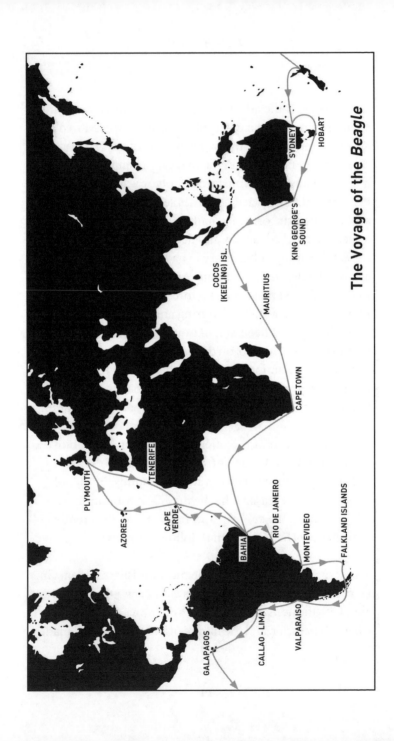

The Voyage of the *Beagle*

up his mind. He was unequivocal: Charles should join the *Beagle* voyage. The uncle could see what the father could not. Charles' future lay as much with science as with the Church. The *Beagle* voyage was not to be feared: 'Looking upon him as a man of enlarged curiosity, it affords him such an opportunity of seeing men and things as happens to few.'[36] Darwin, in agonies of excitement and projected regret, sent the news back to the Mount: '… may I beg of you one favour? It will be doing me the greatest kindness, if you will send me a decided answer, yes or no.'[37]

Jos had spoken in favour of the trip, and that was enough for the doctor. He kept to his word and gave his blessing. Quite suddenly, all was well. With the family now backing the project, haste was necessary to cement the arrangements. Darwin wrote a formal letter to Francis Beaufort, head of the Hydrographer's Office, accepting the offer, and immediately set off for London to meet FitzRoy. He found the captain generous and helpful, and admired FitzRoy's manner of coming straight to the point.[38] He was, he told Henslow, 'everything that is delightful'.[39]

The two men headed for the London arcades together, bound by their looming adventure and their shopping lists. Rattling from place to place in FitzRoy's carriage, Darwin realised that the aristocratic commander would be an extraordinary companion in all respects. His wealth – and his inclination to spend it as required and without hesitation – was remarkable. Darwin was astonished to see £400 spent just on FitzRoy's guns and started to wonder about his own equipment. He took advice from

Henslow and Sedgwick on the diverse issues of collecting: what types of spirit, bottles and pins should he bring? He was told which books to pack, and how best to prepare a skin for packing and posting. Letters streamed home to the Mount, asking for shirts to be made up and for his room to be ransacked for a few favourite possessions. All this was utterly engrossing, and the detailed, urgent work no doubt pushed away uncomfortable thoughts about the enormity of the experience that lay ahead: 'It is such capital fun ordering things, today I ordered a rifle and two pairs of pistols, for we shall have plenty of fighting with those d——— cannibals.'[40] Back in Shrewsbury, the doctor leaned over his desk and began to write the cheques.

On 27 December 1831, after months of refitting in Plymouth, the *Beagle* set off. Darwin spent the first few days seasick, his feelings of nausea compounded by the cries of several men being flogged for their drunken behaviour on Christmas Day. On 2 January 1832 he wrote in his diary, 'Heavy weather. – I very nearly fainted from exhaustion.'[41] This early encounter with seasickness set the scene for the voyage. Whenever the *Beagle* was in turbulent seas, Darwin suffered. But from the start he had a strategy to cope. He found lying down was the best way to adapt, abruptly abandoning his tasks when the nausea arrived and returning to them when he felt a little better.

Only 90 feet in length, the *Beagle* was extremely robust and seaworthy; thus however fragile his stomach, Darwin could at least feel secure. As the ship bumped its way down the Bay of Biscay he cheered himself up by reading the explorer von

Humboldt's 'glowing accounts' of the tropics. Those jungles, he knew, would make it all worthwhile. Characteristically, in his letters and diary there bobs a constant succession of enthusiasms and triumphs, as he set about his task as the on-board scientist. He had the habit of noticing his surroundings, and was forever jotting comments:

> There was a glorious sunset this evening and is now followed by an equally fine moonlight night. – I do not think I ever before saw the sun set in a clear horizon. I certainly never remarked the marvellous rapidity with which the disk after having touched the ocean dips behind it.[42]

The crew noticed his energy and respected him. They called him 'Philosopher'.

The *Beagle* called at the arid and volcanic Cape Verde islands, where Darwin had his first experience of the tropics. Seeing him so delighted by the island of St Jago, FitzRoy thought Charles was like a child with a new toy. Then, some eight weeks after leaving Plymouth, the *Beagle* began its approach to Brazil. The town of Bahia rose up from the horizon, a low line of buildings pressed in by the forest, its detail snapping into focus. The ship drew into the bay of All Saints, 'scattered over with large ships'.[43] The elegant white town houses contrasted wonderfully with the deep green of the forest looming behind. Darwin was straight away enchanted and at the earliest opportunity he nosed his way into a section of forest. He was in heaven; he told his diary, 'To a person fond of Natural history such a day as this brings with it pleasure more acute than he may ever again experience.'[44] He rented a house and settled in for an extended stay.

It was time to write to Henslow. Six months had passed – six memorable and productive months. St Jago had been rather barren of life, Darwin said, but the geology was 'preeminently interesting'. His collecting was prodigious and, by and large, the ship life suited him. Having visited both Bahia and Rio de Janeiro, Charles could assure his friend that, just as von Humboldt had said, the rainforest was sublime: 'Nothing, but the reality can give any idea, how wonderful, how magnificent the scene is.'[45] Henslow, who was to receive a constant supply of news from Darwin over the coming months and years, took extracts from the letter, read them to the Cambridge Philosophical Society and later published them as a pamphlet.

Darwin knew that he should keep a diary for eventual publication, but his letters home had more immediate impact. Those written to Henslow went beyond mere friendly notes: they were one half of a conversation between Darwin and his mentor, as they argued over the significance of the specimens being sent from the *Beagle*. Henslow, in turn, spread the news, so that, as the voyage continued, the reports from the *Beagle* began to grab the attention of scientists in Cambridge and across the land. Darwin might be sailing further and further from England, with no time set for his return, but as a man of science he was journeying steadily towards the centre.

5

New Thoughts

While on board HMS *Beagle*, as naturalist, I was much struck with certain facts in the distribution of the inhabitants of South America, and in the geological relations of the present to the past inhabitants of that continent. These facts seemed to me to throw some light on the origin of species – that mystery of mysteries ...

Charles Darwin, 1859[46]

The *Beagle* voyage was Darwin's critical experience, the episode that shaped his life as well as his theory of evolution. He was on a great adventure and everything was fresh and vivid. His diaries, his notebooks and his letters home are filled with enthusiastic descriptions of the marvels of nature he saw everywhere around him. In everything he wrote during those days there is a feeling of high excitement; this is a young man who at last has found his focus.

Yet there was no single moment of inspiration on the voyage when he decided that species evolve, one from another. Even his visit to the Galapagos Islands, often seen as the place where Darwin first witnessed evolution in action, did not trigger an immediate cascade of understanding in his mind. His priority was to collect as much as possible.

During those years of South American exploration, it was Captain FitzRoy's habit to deposit his friend on land while he made his measurements of the coast. Darwin would go to the nearest bank to cash another cheque from his father's account, then set off exploring with his assistant and equipment. Sometime later the *Beagle* would call in at a coastal town or city, pick up Darwin and his boxes, and move on.

Every scientist has a personal style and Darwin developed his particular way of working while on the *Beagle*. More than many scientists, he liked to mix the formal and the informal, the imaginative and the measured. Travelling inland, he jotted down in a series of notebooks magically evocative descriptions of his surroundings. It is easy to imagine him in the rainforest, with his assistant, breathlessly chasing down some animal, shouting with excitement.

Back on board the *Beagle* the formal work would begin. Cramped into his cabin, he made lists and annotations, checked names against his textbooks and continued his background reading. Above all, he wanted to cement his reputation with Henslow, and wrote frequently to remind Henslow that his ceaseless collecting was building a treasure trove that would keep the scientists back home in England busy for years. In the first letter he went out of his way to suggest he was almost overwhelmed by what he was seeing, and was unsure what was significant and what was not: 'One great source of perplexity to me is an utter ignorance whether I note the right facts, and whether they are of sufficient importance to interest others. In the one thing, collecting, I cannot go wrong.'[47] For the next few years Henslow experienced Darwin's collecting zeal through the deliveries of crated specimens arriving for inspection at his London home.

Yet he wasn't simply hammering, shooting and pickling. The young Darwin was a thinking man. Newly trained in geology, as he travelled he pondered the history of the rock formations he saw around him, their age and their origins. He was interested, too, in the lively debates then under way about the history of animals and plants on the planet. Partly this was a family affair: his grandfather Erasmus was famous for his poetic writings about the origin of species. But he also contemplated those difficult days in Edinburgh, and his zoology instructor Robert Grant. In Paris, Grant had known the French evolutionist Lamarck, and shared his belief that species changed over time. Grant and Darwin must have discussed the 'species question' as they traversed the cold beaches of the Forth. As Darwin trawled through his past experience and multiplied his knowledge through daily collecting, he was getting ready to address the question he knew to be the biggest in all of natural history – the origin of all the Earth's species.

The idea prevalent in the 1830s, supported by Henslow and others, was that the origin of species was a theological and not a scientific question. As suggested by the Bible in the Book of Genesis, species were 'fixed'. Perhaps they could vary a little over the generations, but not by much, and certainly not by enough to become a new species. No, when new species formed – and at the start of the nineteenth century the fossil record was beginning to make clear that new species were indeed formed from time to time – some creative force was needed. This force, someone like Henslow would believe, was the designing God – the same God that Darwin, a priest-in-waiting studying the divine creation in South America, was planning to represent to some rural community.

A key text Darwin had studied in Cambridge was Rev. William Paley's *Natural Theology, or Evidences of the Existence and Attributes of the Deity*, published in 1802. Paley, seeing the marvellous way in which animals and plants were so finely adapted to the environment, invoked the metaphor of a watch found in a field. Did not the mechanism of a watch reveal the work of a designer of the utmost skill, he asked. Further, with living beings so exquisitely adapted to their environment – an intricacy of design far beyond the dreams of any clockmaker – was this not proof of a benevolent and creative deity? The Darwin who set sail in the *Beagle* from Plymouth was inclined to share Paley's view, and had even memorised long passages from the book.

Yet, reading in his cabin, Darwin knew that geologists were dramatically lengthening their estimated age of the Earth. Their work was throwing up a fatal challenge to any literal biblical account of creation, which reckoned life to be only a few thousand years old. Moreover, the fossils geologists were splitting from rocks revealed evidence of species extinction as well as the emergence of new forms. Why did species go extinct? And how were new species formed? As the *Beagle* continued its voyage, it was a question that began to nag with increasing frequency at Darwin's mind.

The main scholarly influence on Darwin's thinking at this time was Charles Lyell's book *The Principles of Geology* (Henslow had insisted he take a copy with him on his voyage). Lyell was a young lawyer and geologist.

His own travels included a visit to Mount Etna in Sicily, where he observed that the mountain was built up of many layers of cooled lava. He concluded that the mountain had been formed by a series of steady volcanic processes, on the same scale as current seismic events. Less dramatic geological processes seemed to follow a similar pattern. Lyell pointed out that given enough time a stream threading its way down a valley would etch deep into the hardest rock. This vision of slow, small actions producing some of the grandest features of the planet had a profound impact on Darwin. He began to apply Lyell's thinking to every geological conundrum he encountered. Fossil seashells high in the Andes were explained by the seabed being forced slowly upwards as landmasses were elevated. And those coral reefs that fringed the islands of the Pacific, and whose calcium foundations reached to astonishing depths in the ocean, were simply reaching for the light as the seabed slowly sank. Later, as the *Beagle* began its return journey to England, Darwin began to transfer Lyell's method from rocks to living things. Could species, too, be shifting as the world changed?

In September 1832, its survey of the Brazilian coastline complete, the *Beagle* pushed south into the colder waters of Argentina. One day, sailing with FitzRoy in a small boat close to the shore, Darwin noticed some very large bones jutting out from some low cliffs. A week of excavation followed, Darwin bringing on board and laying on the deck great mounds of soil for sifting, together with some colossal bones. It was clear straightaway that these were fossils of some truly huge creatures – probably including a *Megatherium*, Darwin thought. The size was dramatic and novel but the familiarity of the bones was just as thought provoking. These giant sloths, though extinct, were similar to the living small sloths Darwin could see in the rainforest. Judging by the embedding strata, the fossils were not very old. Darwin duly packed them up and sent them back to Henslow. When Darwin finally returned to England, these fossil bones became an important spur to Darwin's developing ideas on the formation of new species.

The *Beagle* spent some two years on the eastern coast of South America, before it moved round the tip of the continent and over to the west coast in July 1834. Darwin spent much of this period ashore, exploring and collecting. Apart from being laid out at one point by a debilitating and mysterious illness, serious enough to alarm Captain FitzRoy, he remained largely in good health; he was a martyr to seasickness, but was otherwise strong and robust, and a good person in an emergency. His decisiveness became plain one day on the Chilean coast. The ship's company had gone ashore on small boats and were enjoying a pause on the beach. Just 200 yards away, a towering cliff of ice formed a remarkable backdrop to their evening picnic. Suddenly the whole face of the cliff split from the main body and fell crashing into the sea, sending up a tidal wave that rushed towards the resting men. Darwin and a few others saw that the waves would sweep up the coast and drag their small boats out to sea or simply smash them. They sprinted down the sands and hauled the boats further up the beach, just in time to save them. It was a close call and FitzRoy was impressed. The next day, sailing into a large spread of water, he named it 'Darwin Sound'.

Darwin's ideas were beginning to gel. Wherever he looked he saw evidence of a planet in transition. He became increasingly persuaded by Lyell's vision of slow and constant change as the genesis of the Earth's contours. More evidence came his way in 1835, when he experienced an earthquake. 'The most awful yet interesting spectacle I ever beheld,' he noted in his diary on 5 March. FitzRoy visited an island close to the epicentre and found that the earthquake had raised its ground level by 8 feet.

The world was on the move, Darwin saw. But what about biology? How did the organic world respond to this constant transition? Lyell was clear on the matter. A species went extinct, he wrote, because it couldn't adapt to the environment changing around it, even over millions of years. But how could new species be formed? On this Lyell was quiet, merely admitting that species would have to be 'created'. Darwin, alone with his ideas, began to wonder whether a more natural explanation could be found – that as the planet shifted so the constellation of species to be found on Earth shifted too.

The final South American destination for the *Beagle* was the Galapagos, an archipelago of volcanic islands 600 miles off the coast of Ecuador along the equator, and Darwin greatly looked forward to the landing. He had heard that there were volcanoes still active on the islands, and he knew of the strange beasts that lived there – especially the giant tortoises. For three hot and thirsty weeks he moved from island to island, observing the extraordinary wildlife but unsure quite what to make of it. In particular, Darwin saw two things that he only half understood, but which were in time to spark his evolutionary thinking. First were the giant tortoises. A local British diplomat told him that each island had its own type of tortoise and that by looking at the carapace of these lumbering beasts it was possible to identify which island it came from. The second phenomenon concerned the island finches, which also varied greatly across the archipelago. Only later did the significance of these facts become clear in Darwin's mind.

Leaving the Galapagos, the *Beagle* set sail for England, via New Zealand and South Africa. It took a year to get home, with the painstaking FitzRoy insisting on a final crossing of the Atlantic to check longitude. The *Beagle* arrived in Falmouth, England on 2 October 1836. Darwin left the ship immediately and took the coach for Shrewsbury, arriving at the Mount in the middle of the night. It was heaven to be home, and he sent his first letter neither to Henslow nor to a friend, but to the wise relative who had made it all possible, Jos Wedgwood: 'My dear Uncle … I reached home late last night … I cannot allow my sisters to tell you first … I am so very happy I hardly know what I am writing.'[48]

6

New Scientist

I have read some short papers to the geological Soc, and they were very favouribly [sic] received by the great guns, and this gives me much confidence, and I hope not a very great deal of vanity; though I confess I feel too often like a peacock admiring his tail. I never considered that my geology would ever have been worth the consideration of such men as Lyell, who has been to me since my return a most active friend.

Charles Darwin, letter to William Fox,
7 July 1837[49]

Arriving at the Mount late at night after a two-day coach journey, Darwin had gone straight to bed without waking anyone. The following morning he walked in unannounced at breakfast. The traveller was 27 years old and had been away for five years. As the stories began to be recounted, and the doctor scrutinised his returning child, everyone could see he was flourishing. Caroline, writing almost immediately to the Wedgwoods, describes a family reunion where the joy was complete: 'We have had the very happiest morning – poor Charles so full of affection and delight at seeing my father looking so well.' Beyond her delight at her brother's return, she saw that the *Beagle* was the crucible that had transformed her wandering brother into someone with a clear direction: 'He has gained happiness and interest for the rest of his life.'[50]

The family now understood beyond all doubt that science was the element animating Darwin's future. They already knew that Henslow had been spreading the word about Darwin's *Beagle* work and that prestigious scientists were giving it their approval. Just recently Adam Sedgwick, the man who had tutored Charles in field geology, had visited the Mount and told the assembled Darwin clan that the absent son would soon 'take a place among leading scientific men'.[51] Dr Darwin, that shrewd judge of people, saw the solidity of his son, and appreciated his growing reputation. As a doctor he understood personality, but it was as a banker that he understood risk, and the *Beagle* adventure looked set to be among his best investments. Settling into old age, Robert Darwin could look on his vigorous son with pride. For five years he had read with a mix of pleasure and anxiety Charles' letters home, and he knew that the crates of specimens, some piled up in Cambridge, some still to be disembarked from the *Beagle*, contained the raw materials for a long and systematic study. Those rocks and skins, he knew, would project Charles forward into a life of profitable labour. There was no question of his son falling into lazy, costly inactivity.

Just as the doctor had financed a residency on the *Beagle*, so now he would extend his patronage forward to a period in London, to Charles' marriage in 1839, and to the eventual purchase of a handsome home on the Kent chalk grasslands in 1842. Though an established and respected scientist from the moment he arrived back in England, it was many years before Charles earned money from his endeavours. He never forgot the doctor's generosity and the enduring significance of a supportive father; with his own children, too, he was always attentive and scrupulous. All the letters home from the *Beagle* ring with filial gratitude. 'Give my love to my dear Father,' he once told Caroline. 'I often think of his kindness to me in allowing me to come [on] this voyage – indeed in what part of my life can I think otherwise.'[52] During his travels, as Charles drew out cash from banks across the globe, splashing out on provisions and horses as necessary, and even retaining an assistant on board the *Beagle*, he had plenty of evidence that all was well with the family finances.

For now, free of the *Beagle*, Darwin was back in Shropshire and surrounded by adoring and admiring family and friends. Yet taking a rest was the last thing on his mind. 'A man who dares waste one hour of time, has not discovered the value of life,'[53] he once told his sister Susan – a sentiment central to his working life. In truth, the last period on board the *Beagle* had dragged, especially when FitzRoy had made his unexpected final detour across the Atlantic. By then Darwin's mind was on the future, and he was desperate to be home. The family duly received a vexed letter about a delay that '… has put the finishing stroke to my feelings. I loathe, I abhor the sea, and all ships which sail on it.'[54] Back on land at the Mount, he could at last take charge of his affairs, push forward his science and make his name.

First he had to decide where to live. Over in Cambridge Henslow was husbanding Darwin's crates and was eager to see his favoured student. Cambridge was attractive for its quiet: now that Darwin was enchanted by the magic of scientific explanation, and his collecting days were over, the company of university professors might be valuable. Yet he doubted he wanted to settle there. Down in London there was the witty and cultured Erasmus with his comfortable lodgings and articulate friends: a good prospect after the *Beagle*. It would also be exciting finally to meet his geological hero, Charles Lyell. In London, too, there was the range of experts he needed to help him sort and identify his specimens, the colleagues who would build the backbone of a vast work of description, which in the end took ten years to complete. If he lived in London it would be easier to flatter, hire or simply twist the arms of ornithologists, entomologists and other scientists. The allure of metropolitan science was irresistible. After a few months criss-crossing the country, travelling between Shropshire and Cambridge, Darwin made his apologies to Henslow: 'I assure you I grieve to find how many things make me see the necessity of living for some time in this dirty odious London.'[55] How horribly ironic, he thought, that such a place, devoid of nature, is where the experts pursue natural history. He soon grew to hate the city, telling his Cambridge friend Fox – now settled in the Isle of Wight – that London was a pit of 'smoke, ill health and hard work'.[56]

Darwin lived in London for five years, working at a frantic pace. He joined the committee of the Geological Society, and settled to the enormous task of getting his collections properly examined, interpreted and written up. Most immediately there was his *Beagle* diary to sort through, edit and publish. FitzRoy, too, had kept a journal, and the two accounts were published together, Darwin's joyous and entertaining version being immediately the more successful. Of course Darwin saw his book as a scientific account, but he was delighted that his lively prose was bringing him admirers. The most perceptive reader's comment sprang from the eminent geologist William Henry Fitton. The science was good, he said, but so was the sensibility: 'What I like best is the tone of kind and generous feeling that is visible in every part, so that one sees that it is the work of a plain English gentleman travelling for information and not for effect, and viewing all things kindly.'[57] Such praise encouraged Darwin and he never forgot the feeling. Later, in his autobiography, he wrote that 'The success of this my first literary child always tickles my vanity more than that of any of my other works'.[58]

Darwin was clarifying his view on the matter that was to shape his life – the transmutation of species. He nonetheless stayed silent on the subject. By the end of the *Beagle* voyage, he had come to the conclusion, against scientific orthodoxy, that new species formed from pre-existing ones. In London, Darwin must have felt lonely with his idea. Even his hero Lyell, writing about extinction, believed in the fixity of species. Lyell knew that species went extinct but declared that the new species which followed were mysteriously created as necessary, fresh each time. Cautious about discussing his ideas openly, Darwin started instead to keep a series of notebooks in which he jotted things down as they came to him. These 'transmutation notebooks' – a diminutive library of scribbled thoughts – became the place where Darwin stabilised his tumbling ideas and searched for the best way to express his theory.

Darwin's career of secret reflections received a helpful jolt in March 1837 when the ornithologist John Gould reported back to him about those strange Galapagos birds he had collected. They were all finches, Gould said, but of different species, and unique to the islands. With Gould's expertise at his side, Darwin could now ponder more systematically the origin of different life forms on the islands. To his mind the evolutionary explanation was compelling. Knowing the Galapagos to be volcanic and formed in the recent geological past, Darwin conjectured that the finches had flown there from mainland Ecuador, as a flock and all of one species. Over time, the single stock must therefore have diverged, slight varieties becoming more and more distinct, the process becoming strengthened as populations separated to the different islands. Eventually, Darwin saw, the differences would become significant enough to make them separate species.

Another spur to Darwin's thinking emerged from the giant fossils of huge extinct mammals he had unearthed with FitzRoy in South America, and which he had put in the hands of the eminent palaeontologist Robert Owen. It was clear, said Owen, that the bones were of extinct animals, but it was also clear that the giant fossils were similar in form to some of the small animals – sloths and armadillos – now roaming the same landscapes. This was no coincidence, Darwin realised: the simple fact was that the newer forms of these mammals were derived from the older forms. In Darwin's phraseology, it was a fine example of 'descent with modification'.

Darwin's notebooks filled as he wrestled with the implications of the Galapagos birds and the South American fossils. Aware that the power of persuasion is a vital attribute for any scientist, he was also looking for a way of explaining evolution to a wider public as well as seeking a way of writing about the origin of species that would convince his scientific colleagues. He knew he had to be careful: the French biologist Jean-Baptiste Lamarck's well-known views on the progressive change of species were derided by British scientists, and so by implication was the idea of evolution. Without a clear thesis, plausible in structure and well supported by recognised evidence, men like Lyell and Henslow would persist in their belief that the origin of species was simply an intractable mystery, with divine action a possible underlying cause.

What Darwin needed was a mechanism – a way to explain how new species, descending from those going extinct as the environment slowly shifted, could fit the new conditions so well. It was the marvellous adaptation of living things that made Paley's theory of a designer god so compelling an idea, alluring even to Darwin in his Cambridge years. Urgently he asked himself: what makes newly evolved species so well designed? If God is not the cause of new species' precise 'fit' to their environment, what is?

The answer came in September 1838, when Darwin read the work of Thomas Malthus, an economist worried about England's growing population. Left unchecked, Malthus said, a human population would double in twenty-five years. Population control, in the Malthusian scheme, was caused by famine, disease and war, so attempts to mitigate such 'natural' suffering would have frightening consequences in terms of population growth. As Darwin read this, in his mind's eye he saw not the Victorian poor, but any natural population. Did animals not produce more offspring than ever reached maturity? What would happen to an elephant population if it were left 'unchecked'? He saw that populations tend to stay stable because they are constrained by the fierce natural parameters of predation, limited food and habitat. But what precise conditions would decide which creatures would die and which would survive – or be 'naturally selected'? In any population of creatures from the same species, individuals vary. As he later wrote: 'No one supposes that all the individuals of the same species are cast in the same mould.'[59] They varied, one from another, in myriad small ways. Variation is obvious in domestic animals, like dogs, but it exists equally in non-domesticated species. Moreover, Darwin was aware that this variation was very often inherited by the offspring. From his knowledge of animal breeding, he knew that the specialist characteristics of a dog or a pigeon variety will run down through the generations. The same process is found throughout nature, he said. In the Darwinian scheme, all living things produce more offspring than can survive. With limited food, and with disease and predation a constant pressure, there will be some individuals better placed to survive and breed. These individuals are therefore 'naturally selected' and pass on their favourable characteristics to their young; these too are more likely to survive. In time, especially if all the while the environment is changing, a new species will form.

At last, three years after leaving the *Beagle*, Darwin had a theory by which to work. It wasn't complete, and it wouldn't convince his friends, but he knew the framework was robust. Careful, meticulous and in no rush to publish, Darwin now developed a strategy of research that would generate the data and the concepts needed to bolster his theory. He would dig deep, and go back and forth across the terrain of natural history. Over many years he built up a network of correspondents across the world: scores of scientists, collectors and animal breeders who could provide him with the breadth and depth of information necessary for building a new view of life. To bring that amount of care to the work, he knew, would take fortitude and patience. So his immediate objective was to keep on building a professional identity, to become an established figure in the London scientific community. It was better to bide his time than risk a premature announcement that might alienate his colleagues.

Darwin was also alert to the way theories about evolution and politics link up. These were times of huge and often frightening social unrest. The nation's wealth was growing, along with its expanding industry, making unsustainable the rigid control of parliament by landowners and a restricted electorate. The Reform Acts of the 1830s widened the franchise, but progress was slow and political dissidence pulsed through England.

The Darwin family and the Wedgwoods backed political reform, but the unrest could be frightening. Lamarck's ideas offered apparent backing for the idea of sudden upward social mobility. Darwin had no desire to have his embryonic ideas swept into a vortex of political turmoil and be damned for the wrong reasons.

7

Marriage

I marvel at my good fortune that she, so infinitely my superior in every single moral quality, consented to be my wife. She has been my wise adviser and cheerful comforter throughout life ...

I have indeed been most happy in my family, and I must say to you my children that not one of you has ever given me one minute's anxiety, except on the score of health. There are, I suspect, very few fathers of five sons who could say this with entire truth. When you were very young it was my delight to play with you all, and I think with a sigh that such days can never return.

Charles Darwin[60]

While Darwin struggled in silence with his theory of evolution, another idea began to take root: he found himself thinking of marriage. Wholly consumed by his scientific projects, he was becoming aware of the dangers of overwork. It was exciting that the *Beagle* research was steadily propelling him deep into the London web of professional science, but the effort of managing the project was enormous. Even with Erasmus' dinner parties, and friendly invitations to scientific gatherings, something was missing from life. As he told a friend, 'We poor bachelors are only half men – creeping like caterpillars through the world, without fulfilling our destination'.[61]

Darwin was also aware of another, more sinister problem. His health had recently become alarmingly variable. No longer was he the robust mariner who raced down beaches or picked his way through the passes of the Andes. These days he was troubled by nausea, stomach pains and dreadful headaches, and even rashes and eczema. Within a year of his return to England he was complaining to Henslow about his frailty: 'Anything which flurries me completely knocks me up afterwards.'[62] A pattern was emerging – a constant theme of his life – of prolonged, chronic ill health. He saw the cause as overwork, stress or sudden exertion. And with the ill health came pessimism, that for all his gifts, there was a fundamental bodily weakness that could at any time lay him low, perhaps even kill him.

Darwin could see that the question of marriage should not be shelved. Procrastination might be a sensible policy for his theory of evolution; matrimony, by contrast, was a matter of commitment. Characteristically, he decided to make some notes on the issue and in July 1838 compiled two lists, one for the advantages, the other for the disadvantages of the married state. On the positive side, he let himself imagine a chatty 'nice soft wife on a sofa with good fire, and books and music perhaps'. On the negative side, if work was one's destiny, marriage must mean a 'terrible loss of time'. And with marriage there would be anxiety and responsibility. Certainly 'he would never go up in a balloon, or take solitary trips in Wales'. But, having seen how stressed he was already as a result of his workload, he knew it wasn't good to spend one's whole life 'working like a neuter bee'. The prospect of monkish labour was awful: 'Imagine living all ones days solitarily in smoky dirty London house!' he scribbled.[63] In any case, the company of women was important and enjoyable to him. During the Cambridge years he'd spent delightful months flirting with Fanny Owen, a family friend, and though the *Beagle* was as male as life could get, he'd hugely enjoyed his sisters' letters, with their constant stream of news about romantic entanglements, marriages and babies. Pondering his lists, Charles was aware that back in

Shropshire the sisters, too, were conjuring up his future, their letters a reminder, if it were needed, that there is more to life than science.

Darwin, notably articulate and honest about his feelings, could see what he should do. At the end of those comforting and orderly lists he scribbled his decision: 'marry – marry – marry.' But when? Sooner rather than later, his father had advised. According to Dr Darwin, the feelings of youth are livelier. No doubt thinking of his own dear dead Susannah, the father counselled the son: why delay happiness?

Darwin's sisters had someone already in mind: Emma Wedgwood. Charles and Emma were cousins, as Susannah had been Emma's aunt. It was Emma's father, Josiah Wedgwood – shooting partner of the teenage Charles – who had been instrumental in sanctioning the *Beagle* trip by reassuring the doctor of its value. Closer still, Darwin's sister Caroline had married Joe Wedgwood, Emma's older brother. The families were remarkably intertwined; a marriage between Charles and Emma would therefore seem entirely normal – the continuation of a family habit.

Charles and Emma had known each other for years, of course. And meeting up again after the *Beagle* years they found new interest in each other. Emma was frankly impressive. Sophisticated and passionate about politics, steeped in the liberal politics of the Wedgwoods and robustly opposed to slavery, she campaigned for her father when he became the first Member of Parliament for Stoke-on-Trent. She was a linguist, an excellent pianist, energetic and well-read. She knew her mind and had already turned down suitors.

Charles, obsessed with work, ambivalent about the social circuit and preferring scientific to political discussion, might have wondered whether Emma, so articulate and lively and interested in everything, would accept him. Did he even have the courage to propose? He had tried to simplify the marriage question into a list, but now he must take the risk and ask her for her hand. He needn't have worried. In the aftermath of his homecoming there had been enough meetings between the two of them for Emma to see his virtues and imagine him as a husband. She had been delighted by his good manners and honest nature. As she once said, 'He is the most open, transparent man I ever saw and every word expresses his real thoughts'.[64] When Darwin finally brought himself to propose marriage, she accepted immediately. It seemed the most natural thing in the world.

Charles and Emma moved into a house in Upper Gower Street, in Bloomsbury, London, in early 1839. Country people to the core, they tolerated London for one reason only: it was the site of Darwin's science. He was a pillar of the learned societies, a celebrated explorer of the world and – with Emma was at his side – a busy subscriber to the give and take of social life. But marriage had not put paid to Darwin's symptoms, and all too often a late night or enthusiastic debate would leave him 'knocked up'. The needs of Emma's ailing mother at the Wedgwood house in Staffordshire, and Darwin's trips to the Mount, added to the demands placed on the couple. The only way Darwin got any relief from his symptoms was to view with extreme suspicion any social exertion. To make the point that he was a poor prospect for dinner parties, his letters are peppered with references to his sorry state. As he told his dear friend William Fox: 'I am forced to live very quietly and am able to see scarcely anybody and cannot even talk long with my nearest relations.'[65] The domestic toil was growing too, with the birth of his first children, William in 1839 and Annie in 1841. Charles and Emma made up their mind: London was not for them, or for their 'little chickens'. With huge relief – and the doctor's money – they bought a house in the Kent village of Downe and moved there in late 1842, a few weeks before the birth of their third child, Mary. With a country house and a new baby, Darwin was delighted: 'We are going on very well and Emma is making a quicker recovery, owing I think to country air, than she has ever done before.'[66]

The new home, called Down House, was Darwin's haven – a cradle for developing his theories of evolution. After the hectic intellectual pace of London life, he now sought a calmer routine. When he looked from his study windows he saw his garden and space for his children to play. A little to the side of the garden were the large beds for vegetables, supervised by Emma. In time, at the far border of his land, he would plant a small wood, skirted by the 'Sandwalk' – the path he took at the start of each day. (When the children were grown one of their favourite memories was of their father heading down this path, his stick tapping against the flints, as he gathered his thoughts and prepared for the day's work.)

Within the house his children played noisily, and were likely to charge into his study. Darwin was always fascinated by them, doting on them, anxious at every sign of malady. And always there was the emotional and intellectual presence of Emma, who kept the home in equilibrium. Certainly there were tensions, for Emma was a devout Christian who knew her husband was slowly losing his faith. It was also a failing of the doctor and of Erasmus, she reflected, so Charles was not alone among the secular-minded menfolk in the family. Yet his work, she saw, had a particular touch to it, removing the divine from nature. Was there any room left for God? Or, to put it another way, with a gaze as penetrating as her husband's, did science leave anything untouched? She had written to him soon after their engagement, urging him to keep his sense of mystery: 'May not the habit in scientific pursuits of believing nothing till it is proved, influence your mind too much in other things which cannot be proved in the same way, and which if true are likely to be above our comprehension.'[67] It was a letter Darwin kept safe, with a comment scribbled at the end: 'When I am dead, know that many times, I have kissed and cryed [sic] over this.'

Darwin kept the details of his theory of natural selection hidden away, but, by his questions, friends and correspondents could sense his interest in the origin of species. For while Darwin relied on quietude for his research and writing, he thrived on scientific conversation. Within the creative and secure atmosphere of Down House, Darwin felt able to attempt a properly composed account of his theory, and by 1844 had written a 200-page essay, which he did not publish, but instead gave to Emma with instructions for it to be published 'in case of my sudden death'.[68] A vivid sign of the completeness of Darwin's thinking by this stage is shown by this essay, whose structure, and even its final sentence, were used almost unchanged when Darwin finally went public in 1859 with his masterwork *The Origin of Species.*

It was inevitable that Darwin, always a communicative scientist, would seek out a supportive colleague as judicious midwife for his theory. He began a correspondence with the botanist Joseph Hooker, who was then 27 years old and who had just returned from his own voyage of scientific exploration. While Darwin saw Lyell as an entrenched advocate of the fixity of species, the youthful Hooker looked as though he might be more sympathetic and helpful. Darwin dropped some heavy hints: 'I think I have found out (here's presumption!) the simple way by which species become exquisitely adapted to various ends.'[69] To this Hooker replied positively, telling Darwin he would like to know more about species change '… as no presently conceived opinions satisfy me on the subject'.[70] Darwin was tremendously encouraged – in his words they were 'fellow labourers'[71] – and before long he gave his essay to Hooker, who picked his through the unfamiliar arguments. Over the coming years Hooker became Darwin's most faithful interlocutor, as well as a vital adviser on botany.

Hooker's most crucial intervention was to challenge Darwin on his understanding of variation. Hooker probed: was Darwin not a geologist venturing into zoology, and thus an amateur? Darwin took up the challenge. Pondering a strange barnacle from the *Beagle* years, he decided he would research the entire *Cirripede* group. The barnacles were as unexplored as any South American coastline, their taxonomy and physiology an acknowledged gap in the zoological firmament. In fact, it had only been in the last few years that zoologists had realised the animals were crustaceans, not molluscs. Here was a good way for Darwin to establish his zoological credentials – he would become a world expert on just one group of invertebrates. He couldn't know that the work would eventually take eight years to complete and become the longest lasting of any of his research projects.

Bolstered by insights about barnacles, his theory grew in substance. As did his family. Emma had her last baby in 1856, making ten in all – a vast brood whom Darwin nurtured with diligence and good humour. The palpable delight and joy Darwin took in his children is one of his most attractive features. But there were disasters too. The worst was the death, aged 10, of his second born, Annie, in 1851. It was a shocking blow and, for Darwin, so cruel as to be a final refutation of any remaining faith in a loving God. Annie's death revealed the world to be, at root, pitiless. If there is goodness it is only there because of people – the sort of goodness, thought Darwin, his Annie had possessed in such abundance. He wrote: 'We have lost the joy of our household, and the solace of our old age: she must have known how deeply we loved her; oh that she could know how deeply, how tenderly we do still and shall ever love her dear joyous face. Blessings on her.'[72]

By 1854, Darwin had finished his barnacles project. With several volumes published, he had gained a deserved reputation as a zoologist of world authority: now he could talk about animals and fossils with equal credibility. Hooker's challenge had paid off. In studying the barnacles so intently, Darwin knew to the depth of his being that in the natural world individuals of the same species varied hugely, according to differing factors, with the variation affecting every aspect of an organism's construction.

Now Darwin was ready to publish on the subject of evolution. He felt sure his theory was defensible. He could describe variation, and he could explain that nature, however pacific it might look from his window, is marked by a tremendous death rate and a struggle to survive. With variation so fundamental an aspect of any population, the survivors would tend to be those with the better fit to their environment. This struggle for survival would be the engine of their evolution, the cause of new species, and the explanation of their splendid and varied adaptations.

Hooker, a frequent guest at Down House and a stalwart of Darwin's correspondence, was completely convinced. Even Lyell could see the strength of Darwin's position. Moreover, as the worldly Lyell warned, there were other scientists thinking about the origin of species, and they might claim the glory. It was time to publish; time to release his theory to the world.

8

Telling the World

The weather is quite delicious. Yesterday, after
writing to you I strolled a little beyond the glade for
an hour and a half and enjoyed myself ... at last I fell
asleep on the grass and woke with a chorus of birds
singing around me, and squirrels running up the
trees and some woodpeckers laughing ...

Charles Darwin, letter to Emma Darwin,
28 April 1858[73]

Knowing that Darwin took his time to get things right, Lyell suggested he start with a simple sketch, which could be published quickly and would secure his priority: 'I wish you would publish some small fragment of your data ... and so out with the theory and let it take date – and be cited – and understood.'[74] That could be done in just a couple of months – easily manageable. Darwin, always alert to the etiquette of science, pondered this, and told Lyell that he disliked the idea of writing for priority. On the other hand, he 'certainly should be vexed if any one were to publish my doctrines before me'.[75] To rush something out, with copious promises about some future monograph, would, he felt, attract sneers: 'It yet strikes me as quite unphilosophical to publish results without the full details which have led to such results.'[76] But Darwin also knew only too well the labour involved in books – writing up this new project in full, following the barnacles effort, might take years. Just when his moment of real triumph seemed within reach, he found himself beset by dilemmas and doubts. 'I am in a peck of troubles,' he wrote sadly to Hooker.[77] It would almost have been better, he thought, if Lyell had never mentioned the subject.

Two years later, in 1858, Darwin, now aged 49, was still faltering. No short article had appeared; instead, stubbornly, he was bent on compiling an enormous work – a multi-volume project that looked set to occupy him for years. Then, in June 1858, a crisis intervened which caused an acceleration of his plans and put him into the hands of John Murray, one of the nation's most accomplished and efficient publishers.

The drama began with crushing force. One morning Darwin opened a letter postmarked as coming from the Malay Archipelago. Inside he found an essay about the origin of species. It was entitled, 'On the Tendency of Varieties to Depart Indefinitely from the Original Type'. The author was a collector he knew slightly: Alfred Russel Wallace. The title alone was alarming enough to a man who thought he had a monopoly on the proper study of evolution. The text, however, was stunning. Word for word, it seemed, Wallace had laid out the principles of Darwin's ideas. The implications were clear and they were horrifying. Wallace had written an article on natural selection, ready for publication, while Darwin, lost in his book, was still silent.

Among the many ideas contained in the article – and expressed with notable lucidity – Darwin read the following: 'If … any species should produce a variety having slightly increased powers of preserving existence, that variety must inevitably in time acquire a superiority in numbers … and occupy the place of the extinct species and variety.'[78] As Darwin put it, writing at once to Lyell for advice, 'Your words have come true with a vengeance that I should be forestalled … I never saw a more striking coincidence. If Wallace had my MS sketch written out in 1842 he could not have made a better short abstract! Even his terms now stand as heads of my chapters.'[79] 'So all my originality, whatever it may amount to, will be smashed,' he wailed to Lyell.[80]

Darwin was caught in a vice. An idea he thought was his, and his alone, now turned out to be shared with another and much younger man. Moreover, this younger man had entrusted the manuscript into Darwin's hands as a safe conduit for publication. For Wallace had written to Darwin with the express hope that he would look over the essay and, if he thought it had merit, send it to Lyell. Darwin saw with horrible clarity that he was to be the midwife of an idea, rather than its parent.

There was worse to follow. On the very day Wallace's letter arrived, one of the daughters, Etty, was taken seriously ill with diphtheria. Then, suddenly, the baby of the family, Charles Waring, aged 18 months, grew hot and feverish with an intensity that terrified Charles and Emma. Very likely it was scarlet fever, which Darwin knew had just killed three children in the village, while others were 'at death's door, with terrible suffering'.[81]

Darwin hardly knew which way to look. In front of him two of his children were mortally ill. Meanwhile he was obsessed by the cataclysm of Wallace's letter. He was desperately aware of his own anguish at losing priority, but he was equally clear that, in terms of discovery, he had got there first. He could point to those years on HMS *Beagle*, the transmutation notebooks, the 1844 essay and all his conversations with Hooker. Most of this had been accomplished while Wallace was still in his teens. Why then should he relinquish priority?

He wrote again to Lyell: 'There is nothing in Wallace's sketch which is not written out much fuller in my sketch copied in 1844 and read by Hooker some dozen years ago.'[82] Get in touch with Hooker, Darwin urged, and ask his opinion. Might there be a solution that restored his priority, but without prejudice to Wallace or to the precepts of good behaviour? Darwin already knew of Wallace and had corresponded with him, once asking him for some wild fowl specimens. He had even acknowledged that they had similar interests, telling Wallace that he could 'plainly see that we have thought much alike and to a certain extent have come to similar conclusions'.[83] Wallace, in short, was a colleague, even if he was on the other side of the world and not part of the inner circle of Darwin's friends.

Wallace was as far from Darwin in terms of family background as he was geographically. He had always had to earn his living. His father, an unsuccessful solicitor, had died in 1834, when Wallace was only 11. He found work as a land surveyor, taking advantage of the growth of the railways. It was a tough, itinerant existence, and Wallace was struck by the inequalities of an industrialising world. He grew up a socialist and a reformer, and saw in science a force for good. He quickly lost his religion, became entranced by entomology and, together with a companion, Henry Bates, decided to sail for the Amazon and a life as a collector. It was during his second major expedition, to the Malay Archipelago, that he began to develop his ideas about the distribution of species, and by extension, their evolution. The climax of his work came during a bout of malarial fever when Wallace, delirious and confined to bed, suddenly saw how a variety might become a new species, were it better placed to survive the incessant destruction of the natural world. This was when he decided to write to Darwin, as someone who knew him slightly and who could be trusted. Isolated in the Far East, Wallace knew he was in no position to navigate his ideas through London's scientific network. He would rely on Darwin.

Darwin was unable to make a decision. The conundrum was too difficult, and his children were too ill. Lyell and Hooker, however, were in decisive mood, and had no intention of letting the problem fester. They were in no doubts about their friend's priority and they swiftly conjured a solution that would settle the matter. What was needed was not a publication but a session at a learned society, where Darwin and Wallace could both be heard. If extracts from Darwin's 1844 paper were read alongside Wallace's remarkable 1858 essay, no reasonable person could doubt the older man's claim or how the history should be written: Darwin got there first and Wallace was a newcomer.

To make the point even clearer, Lyell and Hooker decided to show too that Darwin had not stopped work on his transmutation theories in 1844, but had been pushing ahead steadily, if quietly, ever since. When they read the material at a meeting of the Linnaean Society, on 1 July 1858, they duly included an 1857 letter Darwin had sent to the Harvard scientist Asa Gray, outlining newer aspects of his theory. At the meeting, Lyell and Hooker supervised, reading out the rather lengthy extracts to the assembled fellows. There was no fuss or excitement, and in his annual summary of events at the Linnaean, the president of the society noted: 'The year which has passed has not indeed been marked by any of those striking discoveries which at once revolutionise, so to speak, the department of science on which they bear.'[84]

Darwin was absent from the meeting, mourning baby Robert, who died from scarlet fever on 28 June. As he told Hooker, 'It was the most blessed relief to see his poor little innocent face resume its sweet expression in the sleep of death. Thank God he will never suffer more in this world.'[85] Eight thousand miles away, and unaware of the turmoil he'd provoked, Wallace had no idea of what was happening. Darwin, now, at last saw what he must do: produce a book, and at double speed.

9

On the Origin of Species

I hope to go to the press in early part of next month.
It will be [a] small volume of about 500 pages or so.
I will of course send you a copy. I forget whether I told
you that Hooker, who is our best British botanist and
perhaps best in World is a *full* convert, and is now
going immediately to publish his confession of Faith.

Charles Darwin, letter to Alfred Russel Wallace,
6 April 1859[86]

Darwin had finally woken up. Wallace's letter, and the decisiveness of his truest friends, bumped him into a state of absolute clarity. Now he would write, and write quickly. By drastically cutting much of his beloved detail, Darwin had a new manuscript ready in May 1859. He needed no reminder of the need for urgency and told John Murray, his publisher, that he was 'very anxious to have it published as soon as can be, as to my knowledge two men are already writing more or less on [this] subject'.[87]

Darwin felt this was a book that would reach beyond the community of scientists. 'It may be conceit,' he told Murray, 'but I believe the subject will interest the public and I am sure the views are original.'[88]

The style in which he wrote, and the clarity of his argument, became a priority. He was therefore shocked when the proofs arrived, wailing to Murray, 'How I could have written so badly is quite inconceivable … All I can say is that I am very sorry.'[89] He promised reform: 'I will do my utmost to improve my style.'[90] To Hooker he complained that his days were entirely taken by the 'accursed proofs … I have fairly to blacken them and fasten slips of paper on, so miserable have I found the style'.[91] Indeed, he was so mortified at the number of changes he was demanding that he offered to reimburse the publisher.

At last, he felt able to report to Murray that, after 'infinite trouble', he thought he had the writing 'fairly good and clear'.[92] Suddenly Darwin had to be more open about his theory, roping in family and friends as guides and assistants. Emma had read the chapters as they were written and the whole manuscript was sent to Georgina Tollet, an old friend and an 'excellent judge of style'.[93] Inevitably, with chunks of manuscript streaming through Darwin's network, there were accidents and hiccups. An embarrassed Hooker wrote to tell Darwin that his precious fair copy of the chapter on geological distribution had got into the drawer used for scrap paper by his children – who, of course, suddenly discovered the delights of art. Nearly a quarter of the chapter had disappeared, Hooker confessed. Darwin, who knew about children, was understanding: 'I have the old MS, otherwise the loss would have killed me!'[94]

The writing had to be good, because Darwin wanted – needed – to be persuasive. His overarching aim was to ask his readers to look again at nature. Most of his audience would accept that the Earth was a place of great antiquity and would understand that fossils showed the fact of extinction. They would also accept that new species emerge periodically, each one with a minutely detailed fit between itself and its environment. But *how* did species arise and fit the environment so well? For many, the phenomenon pointed to the hidden actions of a deity, working as designer and guide. Darwin asked his readers to reconfigure such ideas, so that that they put at the centre not a designing God but a principle, 'natural selection', working insensibly and without divine purpose. Among many striking ideas running through his book was the proposition that nature is a place of struggle and death, and that the tranquillity and beauty we choose to see in the natural world is simply our interpretation of it. The countryside is not an arcadia, said Darwin, but a ruthless environment where, if a creative force must be spoken of, it depends on death. No benign God would surely design so brutal a natural world.

This stark reimagining is nowhere better summarised than in the final page of his masterwork:

It is interesting to contemplate a tangled bank, clothed with many plants of many kinds, with birds singing on the bushes, with various insects flitting about, and with worms crawling through the damp earth, and to reflect that these elaborately constructed forms, so different from each other, and dependent upon each other in so complex a manner, have all been produced by laws acting around us.

These laws, taken in the largest sense, being Growth with Reproduction; Inheritance which is almost implied by reproduction; Variability from the indirect and direct action of the conditions of life, and from use and disuse; a Ratio of Increase so high as to lead to a Struggle for Life, and as a consequence to Natural Selection, entailing Divergence of Character and the Extinction of less-improved forms.

Thus, from the war of nature, from famine and death, the most exalted object which we are capable of conceiving, namely, the production of the higher animals, directly follows. There is grandeur in this view of life, with its several powers, having been originally breathed into a few forms or into one; and that, whilst this planet has gone cycling on according to the fixed law of gravity, from so simple a beginning endless forms most beautiful and most wonderful have been, and are being, evolved.[95]

This passage, which summarises 450 pages of writing, puts into the reader's mind an idea that was remarkable in the nineteenth century, and remains powerful to this day. By mentioning the planets, with their orbits set by gravity, he underscores how his project was to make biology, like physics, a fully scientific enterprise. His message is firm: there is no need to invoke God when scrutinising the natural world; there is no need to praise his glory when marvelling at the intricacy of adaptation. Darwin is not saying that God does not exist, merely that we can explain the natural world using ordinary and understandable natural processes.

Yet science, it is often said, works by observation, and here arose Darwin's primary problem. He could describe variation or predation; he could show how geological processes change the form of the earth; he could point at fossils of species long gone. He could even show how the fabled fit of organisms to their environment often reflected a history of adaptation, rather than a one-off act by a benign deity. But with all this, he could not show natural selection occurring in front of our eyes, in the way that one can watch a chemistry or physics experiment unfold.

Darwin starts his book, therefore, by discussing domesticated animals, such as dogs and farm stock. He announces to his readers that he has, 'after deliberation, taken up domestic pigeons. I have kept every breed which I could purchase or obtain ... I have associated with several eminent fanciers and have been permitted to join two of the London Pigeon Clubs.'[96] Why would a scientist who was so well travelled, had studied so much of the natural world and who was famous for the diversity of his research, ranging from the formation of coral reefs to the anatomy of barnacles, seem at such pains, at the start of his book, to convince the reader of yet another expertise – pigeon fancying?

Darwin wanted to show how greatly a species could vary. He knew this from his studies of barnacles, but that was specialist, arcane information. The variation of a single species such as a dog or a pigeon was, by contrast, general knowledge, and thus a better place to start his argument. When one looks at the single species of pigeon, known as the rock dove, Darwin wrote, 'The diversity of the breeds is something astonishing'. He describes in quick order the English carrier, the short-faced tumbler, the pouter, the turbit and the Jacobin. These breeds all look remarkably different from each other: 'If shown to an ornithologist, and he were told that they were wild birds,

[they] would certainly, I think, be ranked by him as well-defined species.'[97] So why, Darwin asks, are these breeds so different even though each of them is descended from the one species? His answer is that they have been specially chosen by breeders and bred for a specific purpose. So it is with all domestic animals. Darwin calls this idea 'artificial selection'.

In nature, too, a species varies. This is the central theme of Chapter 2 of *The Origin*. By talking about pigeons first, and then going on to analyse variations in nature more widely, Darwin is arguing by analogy. He raises in the reader's mind an obvious question: if it is the breeder who selects the 'right' feature to accentuate in the domestic pigeon, who or what takes this role in nature? This is when Darwin comes to the term 'natural selection', and to explain how it works he moves on, in Chapter 3, to what he calls the 'Struggle for Existence'. Using graphic examples, he explains how fast a population of animals can increase and how fierce must be the struggle for life between individuals of the same species, as they compete for space, food and mates. Now he can introduce, in Chapter 4, his great innovation, his theory of natural selection. He has prepared his ground by showing how powerfully and quickly the pigeon breeder can cause changes in his stock. He asks us to think now of the variation that occurs within a natural species. Darwin suggests the hard regime imposed by predation and parasitism, by the need to find food, space and a mate, will select between members of the population. It is a brutal simplicity. If it is a herd of wildebeest or elephants some individuals will have inherited a set of characteristics that give them a better chance in the fierce struggle of life, and so are more likely to survive. By surviving they live to breed and so pass on, through inheritance, the favourable variation.

Darwin reminds the reader of the ever-changing nature of the environment, which results in some varieties inevitably losing their habitat and becoming extinct. Amongst the carnage, however, as time runs out for the less well adapted, others, more favourably endowed, survive and reproduce. Over many generations the survivors show a form or a behaviour differing more and more from the original. In time, over many thousands or many millions of years, the result is a new entity on Earth: a new species.

Darwin saw too that the same process would occur even without some steady shift of the environment, perhaps from cold to warm. Even in the calm meadows familiar to his readers, the animals and plants would always be at risk from any number of hazards, and an individual would always be put at advantage if by chance it developed with some new adaptation, giving it a new and effective way of feeding or designing a nest or finding a mate. Evolution, Darwin was suggesting, will happen anywhere and everywhere, in the 'tangled banks' of the placid English countryside as well as in the remote, gloomy rainforests of the Amazon.

Darwin was delighted to hear from John Murray that the entire print run of 1,250 copies had been taken up by the book trade before publication, and that a further 500 had been ordered by the postal lending library, Mudies. *The Origin*, in other words, was an instant bestseller. Murray made immediate plans for a second edition to be rushed out as soon as possible, and alerted Darwin that he had another opportunity to revise the text. Very likely Murray was relieved that, with the deadline on the second edition so tight, Darwin would have almost no chance to 'blacken the proofs'.

10

After *The Origin*

My dear Sir,
I have sent you a copy of my book (as yet only an abstract) on the Origin of species. I know too well that the conclusion, at which I have arrived, will horrify you but you will, I believe and hope, give me credit for at least an honest search after the truth.

Charles Darwin, letter to James Dwight Dana,
professor of geology at Yale University,
11 November 1859[98]

The effort and anxiety of writing *The Origin* overwhelmed Darwin. Once the final draft was with Murray he set off for a health spa in Ilkley, Yorkshire. Emma and the family arrived two weeks later. The flight from Down House had been forced upon him, he told Hooker: he had been in 'an awful crisis, one leg swelled like elephantiasis – eyes almost closed up – covered with a rash and fiery boils'.[99] Settled in a rented house, but restless as ever, he soon focused once more on his book. *The Origin* was about to be let loose, but he planned to guide its career and give it the best possible start in life. Darwin made one of his long lists and asked Murray to send preview copies to dozens of 'scientific men', colleagues whom he hoped to bring round to his way of thinking. Meanwhile he sent accompanying letters to the same people. All these letters were crafted in a spirit of modesty, but signalled that the author was prepared to defend his work. Darwin knew that few scientists would at once embrace or understand the full scope of his research. Already, with the Linnaean announcement beginning to penetrate the British scientific establishment, battle lines over evolution were being drawn. Relations had cooled with Richard Owen in particular. England's most senior palaeontologist was unimpressed by Darwin's mechanism for evolution: natural selection. Darwin wrote to Owen, warning him that *The Origin* was about to arrive by post: 'I fear that it will be abominable in your eyes; but I assure you that it is the result of far more labour than is apparent on its face.'[100]

Richard Owen had helped Darwin after the *Beagle* voyage, not only with his study of the mammalian fossils from Patagonia, but also with his entry into London's leading scientific circles. Twenty years later he was transforming into a hostile and competitive enemy, and Darwin knew he could expect a curt reply, followed in time by a scathing review in some eminent periodical. It is part of the Darwin story that he was as much a student of scientific politics as he was of evolution itself. For decades he had followed the debates over the origin of life on earth, and seen evolutionary ideas condemned for a great number of reasons: for being atheistic; for naturalising the idea of upward social mobility; for being contaminated by the mystical idea that life has as a primary feature some 'inner desire' to progress.

Darwin wanted to transform the debate by showing that science alone could explain how life evolved. He would show thinking people that the history of life on Earth could reliably be explained as a material process. He admitted there were problems with his theory. There would be things he had got wrong. But these faults and gaps would be a spur to further scientific endeavour, not a reason to jump into the powerful embrace of biblical literalism or to dabble with mystical accounts of life's 'inner force'.

Darwin also knew that the topic of transmutation sold books and had a place in public life. In 1844, fifteen years earlier, a book entitled *Vestiges of the Natural History of Creation* had appeared, by an anonymous author (later identified as the publisher Robin Chambers). *Vestiges* was a huge bestseller. It described the evolution of life on Earth from simple forms to more complex types and even wove humankind into this pattern of progress: people evolving from the apes. Most controversially, all of this was described without reference to divine intervention. When Darwin was writing his book, *Vestiges* was in its tenth edition and still a talking point. Darwin admired its bravura style, even if it played fast and loose with factual detail and was more concerned with the moral implications of evolution than with finding a scientific mechanism.

Darwin saw *Vestiges* as a flawed precursor that had done useful work as a spur to the popular imagination – a book that had shown that evolutionary ideas could now find a place in Victorian society. *Vestiges* helped Darwin frame his book: he too would write for a general readership, and would not be so pompous as to strip out of his writing all signs of spirit and wonder. Yet, even more important to him, he would draw his colleagues into a consensus that his ideas, now at last organised into what he called 'one long argument', could become the fundamental organising principle of biology.

The preview copies had been sent out. Marooned in a freezing Yorkshire, Darwin waited to hear in particular from his three closest advisers. Hooker, the botanist from Kew Gardens, could be relied on: he had been in on the secret for years and was a reliable convert. The renowned geologist Lyell was more problematic. An eminence in British science, he took protocol seriously and moved easily in high society. He knew Darwin's brilliance and, having heard a little of Darwin's ideas, could see their strength. Yet he was conservatively minded and might react adversely to the challenging suggestion that mankind evolved from some ape ancestor.

Finally there was Huxley. Zoologist and anatomist Thomas Huxley, aged only 34, had been Darwin's confidant for nearly a decade. In fighting his way into academia he had developed a bitter antipathy towards entrenched privilege. He wanted science to be truly independent, so that men like him could progress through the merit of their ideas and the force of their work, rather than through a well-provisioned bank account, an affiliation with the Church or acceptance into the prestigious dining clubs at Cambridge. No wonder he became an advocate of science education and a popular orator. Darwin's ideas fed wonderfully into the Huxley vision of the progress of science, albeit that their author was a man of privilege. In the vision of nature projected by *The Origin*, it was science and rationalism, not theology, which provided the tools for the proper understanding of nature.

By the time *The Origin* was published, on 24 November 1859, Darwin knew Huxley's style, and he waited eagerly for his response. All was well: his young friend had been swept away, it seemed. According to Huxley, it had been years since he had been so impressed by a work of science. Boldly he declared that if necessary he was ready to go to battle in support of Darwin's doctrines and that he was 'sharpening up my claws and beak in readiness'.[101]

There followed months of blast and counterblast, with Darwin following the action from Down House. Owen wrote a predictably savage review. Darwin's old teacher Sedgwick told him he had read the book 'with more pain than pleasure ... parts I laughed at till my sides were almost sore ... many of your wide conclusions are based upon assumptions which can neither be proved or disproved'.[102] On the other side, an anonymous but magnificent review in *The Times* cheered Darwin mightily. (It turned out to have been written by Huxley.) But the most famous battle over *The Origin* took place six months later in Oxford.

The British Association for the Advancement of Science met annually, each time choosing a different town, and spent a week learning about and debating the latest science. The meetings aimed to underscore the liveliness of science by highlighting topics of novelty and controversy, and by putting leading scientists in front of popular audiences. Local dignitaries would be on show and journalists often milled around too, looking for stories. In 1860 the British Association met in Oxford. All eyes turned to a session entitled 'On the Intellectual Development of Europe, Considered with Reference to the Views of Mr Darwin'. For all those in search of controversy, this session looked promising. Darwin's latest ideas were known to have strong foes, and some of them would surely be lurking in Oxford. If Huxley were to turn up there was the chance of a memorable, perhaps scandalous, upset. At least 700 people crowded into the hall in the university museum, eager to witness what might transpire.

After a long introductory paper had been read, the Bishop of Oxford took his place on the podium. Samuel Wilberforce was a staunch conservative, as opposed to liberal Anglican tendencies as he was to Darwin's scientific theories. In the heightened atmosphere of the meeting the crowd sensed 'Soapy Sam' might rise to the occasion, and so it proved. He spoke for a good while, parodying Darwinism with witty sarcasm, and he reasserted that the line between animals and humankind was one of nature's boundaries. He declared a turnip could not become a human, and then – as the account has it – he turned to Huxley, who was standing nearby, and asked him whether he claimed to be descended from apes via his grandfather or via his grandmother. Huxley's reply was so superb it passed immediately into folklore:

If I would rather have a miserable ape for a grandfather or a man highly endowed by nature and possessed of great means and influence, and yet who employs those faculties for the mere purpose of

introducing ridicule into a grave scientific discussion
– I unhesitatingly affirm my presence for the ape.[103]

The crowd roared and waited for more, and according to one account, a lady fainted. Others spoke up. Hooker supported Darwin, and explained the relevance of natural selection to botany. FitzRoy, who after the *Beagle* years had become a devout biblical literalist, was seen waving the Holy Book in anger, as if shouting out the Genesis story. Amidst the heat and point-scoring Huxley had made his position icily clear. Whatever might be the current influence of Bishop Wilberforce, it would wane. Science had power, and it was a power that was growing. A decisive moment had been reached: religion was losing its authority as the interpreter of natural history. While this was a philosophical point, Huxley was talking about politics too. His implication was that 'men of power and influence' were a hindrance to society and to progress unless their views accorded with science. Wilberforce and those like him were holding back the march of reason. Here is a battle we have to fight, he was saying: on one side are science and progress, on the other superstition and complacency.

Darwin, secluded in Down House and glad to be a hundred miles away, sent a jokey note to Huxley: 'How durst you attack a live bishop in that fashion? I am quite ashamed of you! Have you no reverence for fine lawn sleeves?'[104] With Huxley and Hooker fighting his corner, he could feel secure. He was liberated now. Telling himself his life's work was done, he directed his gaze with fresh interest at the countryside beyond his study window and pondered the scope of natural selection.

11

Final Years

During subsequent years, whenever I had leisure, I pursued my experiments, and my book on *Insectivorous Plants* was published July 1875, sixteen years after my first observations. The delay in this case, as with all my other books, has been a great advantage to me; for a man after a long interval can criticise his own work, almost as well as if it were that of another person.

Charles Darwin[105]

Tired of books and controversy, Darwin fell in love with orchids. On walks he and Emma had always watched out for these delicate plants, which grew well on the Kent chalk grasslands. Orchids took his attention because of their intricate flowers, designed to draw in insects, which would carry pollen from one plant to another. This cross-pollination, he imagined, would produce the variation that made evolution possible. It would be enjoyable work to look at these flowers in more detail. Typically systematic, Darwin decided to study the whole group, and began to chase up contacts who could send him specimens.

Like his father before him, Darwin enjoyed the quiet space of greenhouses. He duly had a series built along the side of his garden: state-of-the-art structures complete with heating. They were expensive but worthwhile and a delight to Darwin. He sent a cart to Hooker at Kew and it returned with gifts from the national collection. With the boiler stoked up the greenhouses dripped humidity, and Darwin filled them first with orchids, then with other groups whose elaborate habits tugged at his imagination, particularly the insectivorous plants and climbers that trailed along the woodwork. There were memories here of the *Beagle* trip, and his first experience of the tangled rainforest.

The controlled environment encouraged steady work and allowed him to develop his botanical skills. The small world he created in the greenhouse was a relief from the burden of his correspondence. Fiddling around with his experiments, he valued these breaks from writing. 'You can hardly imagine what an interesting morning's work you have given me,' Darwin told an orchid enthusiast he had enlisted as a supplier.[106] But, as ever with Darwin, however much he liked to lose himself in botanical tinkering, his steamy experiments soon had him tending his desk, his reputation and his manuscripts.

Meanwhile, in 1862, Wallace had returned to England, to find the Darwin name firmly linked to the idea they had published together. Ever since Darwin opened Wallace's staggering letter, the co-discoverers had been deeply courteous to each other. Back in London, Wallace showed no grumbles but settled down with his collections and gradually became involved in the metropolitan scientific scene. Darwin, probably a little uneasy at the 1858 arrangement, met Wallace from time to time, and in 1869 described the theory of natural selection as 'your own and my child'.[107] Lyell and Huxley also took Wallace seriously and saw that his understanding of the relation between geography and animal distribution, gained from his immense travels, was unique. In due course, Wallace published his own diary of travels, *The Malay Archipelago*, in 1869, and put as its dedication: 'To Charles Darwin ... as a token of personal esteem and friendship, but also to express my deep admiration for his genius and his works.' His own book on evolution, published in 1889, is called *Darwinism*. If Wallace did feel any rancour it was well concealed.

Darwin suffered a serious decline after he published his orchid work – *On the Various Contrivances by which British and Foreign Orchids are Fertilised by Insects* – in 1862. His health had been fragile ever since his travels, his symptoms arising along with his first inklings of a new explanation for the reality of transmutation. The problem seemed to be centred in his digestive system. It is remarkable how violent, intimidatory and anti-social Darwin's symptoms could be – the antithesis of his own character. Once, when apologising for missing the funeral of John Henslow, he said he was concerned that the sound of his vomiting at night would make him a poor guest.

Of course he was not too ill to enjoy seeing *The Origin of Species* take its position during the 1860s as a dominating explanation of the history of life. He produced new editions as Murray demanded, noted his sales figures with interest and pride, and corresponded amicably (and sometimes irritably) with critics and fans. While his demonstration of the fact of evolution was completely persuasive, the role of natural selection as its chief cause was frequently disputed by scientists, and Darwin was constantly dealing with comments and queries from questioning and sceptical colleagues. It was a public relations campaign he ran from his home, keeping lists of scientists who were opposed and those who were 'converted'. He avoided participating in public debates or lectures, fearing that such exertions would leave him 'knocked up' and unable to work even for an hour a day. His closest allies, Hooker and Huxley, were occasional overnight guests, but they knew that visits to Down House might be cancelled at a moment's notice. Emma saw her husband's torment and knew what was needed. She adjusted life at home to deal with Darwin's anxieties and ill health, framing the day into a strict routine and imposing a wall of quietude around the semi-invalid scientist.

But the ageing Darwin was no sour recluse. His letters ring with life and commitment, both to ideas and to friends. As a rich man, and one of England's premier scientists, he liked to be involved in people's lives. When he heard the sudden news that Robert FitzRoy had committed suicide, he sent a generous cheque to his widow. And at a time when science was barely a profession, with few posts available, he did his best to promote his friends' careers.

All the while book projects were settling in his mind. *The Origin* had been squeezed out of him in haste, thanks to the Wallace crisis, and opened with a reference to the fuller account he hoped one day to write. It was a promise he planned to keep. Once the orchids were out of the way Darwin pressed on with his major statement on evolution: *The Variation of Animals and Plants Under Domestication*, published in 1868, in two volumes.

With the debates about evolution spreading, Darwin's fame multiplied. Scientists and the reading public saw that his theory of natural selection, his style of argument and his convincing scholarship had together produced a decisive moment in the nineteenth-century debate about the history of life. But celebrity also came because, very clearly, his science implied that the evolution of humans could be explained by the same material processes that produced every other creature on the planet. And with this idea, startling to many Victorians, arose another question that preoccupies us to this day: what is the relation between human psychology, or human culture, and our animal past? Or, to put it crudely, are we apes in clothes?

No one could ignore the physical similarity between apes and humans. As Darwin once said, 'Man still bears in his bodily frame the indelible stamp of his lowly origin.'[108] But could biological forces alone account for *Homo sapiens*? When his comrades Lyell and Wallace invoked unknown powers, separate from natural selection, to account for that final triumph of evolution, the human being, Darwin would have none of it. However remarkable the emergence and the final form of advanced human culture (and as a Victorian gentleman it was the European civilisation he had in mind), he refused to accept that any supernatural element had ever been involved. So, how could he talk about the origin of humans without discussing their remarkable mental powers? Was he really going to argue that even human morality was linked to the evolutionary process?

Darwin was cautious on the point. The moral sense, he acknowledged, was by far the most important of all the differences between humans and the lower animals: 'It is the most noble of all the attributes of man, leading him without a moment's hesitation to risk his life for that of a fellow-creature.'[109] Yet he wanted to show that complex human behaviour – morality – did link in some way to behaviour seen in animals. Humans love their dogs, said Darwin, and dogs return their affection 'with interest'.[110] In his *Descent of Man*, published in 1871, Darwin fills page after page with charming accounts of the sympathetic and collaborative attitudes of animals. His examples aimed to make the point that humanity's most exalted feature, '… summed up in that imperious word "ought", so full of high significance', has some representation amongst the animals.[111] We may not be able to derive the details of our moral sense from an understanding of evolution, but that does not mean we have to fall back on 'unknown forces' to explain features that, in some measure, are found elsewhere in the web of life.

Darwin's own morality, as well as his unwavering belief in the power of science, was at stake here. The decade following the publication of *The Origin* had produced the American Civil War, with the northern Union government pledging to end slavery as incompatible with Thomas Jefferson's 1776 Declaration of Independence ('All men are created equal'). It was a war that keenly interested Darwin. With his Wedgwood family background of abolitionists, and his lifelong opposition to slavery, the Union's cause was one he wanted to support. His own weapons in that battle were scientific: he used *The Descent of Man* to fight the idea that the world's races were actually different species, with some forms of human naturally superior.

Darwin was shocked to see his beloved biology being dragooned as support for brutality and discrimination.

The Descent of Man, with calm and measured argument, produces scores of ideas that undermine the multi-species position. In it Darwin reminisces about some of the tribal Fuegians he encountered in South America: 'The Fuegians rank amongst the lowest barbarians; but I was continually struck with surprise how closely the three [Fuegian] natives on board HMS "Beagle", who had lived some years in England, and could talk a little English, resembled us in disposition and in most of our mental faculties.'[112] It was, he suggested, perception, not biology, that separates the peoples of the world. Darwin also pointed out how varied the people of a race may be and reminded his readers how much the peoples of the world interbreed – to produce offspring who are themselves fertile: a sign of being a single species. And he gently satirised the way the multi-species 'camp' could not quite agree on how many human species there may be:

Man has been studied more carefully than any other animal, and yet there is the greatest possible diversity amongst capable judges whether he should be classed as a single species or race, or as two (Virey), as three (Jacquinot), as four (Kant), five (Blumenbach), six (Buffon), seven (Hunter), eight (Agassiz), eleven (Pickering), fifteen (Bory St Vincent), sixteen (Desmoulins), twenty-two (Morton), sixty (Crawfurd), or as sixty three, according to Burke.[113]

Although now old and frail, Darwin continued his research throughout the 1870s, carefully tending his plants and his theories. He died at home on 19 April 1882, with Emma at his side. He was 73. Six months earlier he had published what was to be his last book, an account of the biology of earthworms. True to his style, he wrote there that 'the subject may appear an insignificant one, but we shall see that it possesses some interest',[114] and he delivered insights ranging from observations of the way a worm will plug its burrow to a 'Summary of the part which worms have played in the history of the world'.[115] This celebration of the small and the slow was classic Darwin, his imagination seeing huge significance in the worm casts scattered across his lawn. The obituaries, delivered as often by priests as by journalists and scientists, told the story of a scientist-philosopher who had the discipline needed to succeed at the meticulous craft of science, while having the creativity and vision to change the way we think about ourselves and our relationship with the natural world.

Darwin imagined he would be buried in the village churchyard at Downe, alongside his brother Ras and two of his children. His friends wanted otherwise. Darwin had never been knighted, but surely official recognition of his life and his science could now be arranged. Clergy and politicians agreed, and the clamour in the press, home and abroad, was a reminder of his global importance. The funeral was held at Westminster Abbey on 26 April and Darwin was buried in the nave, next to the astronomer Sir John Herschel. In an unusual collaboration, England's rulers and intellectuals trudged into church together. Wedgwoods and Darwins were there in force too. But Emma remained at home, quiet in the house that Darwin loved. Huxley, Hooker and Wallace, Darwin's best friends and most sympathetic colleagues were among his pallbearers. The great evolutionist was dead, but those supporting him that day in the abbey would carry his new understanding of life into the twentieth century and beyond.

Notes

1   Darwin, Charles, Autobiography in *The Works of Charles Darwin*, Vol. 29 (Pickering & Chatto, 1989), p. 159.

2   Darwin, Charles, *On the Origin of Species by Means of Natural Selection* (Penguin Books, 1968), p. 4538.

3   Autobiography, op. cit., pp. 77–8.

4   Darwin, Erasmus, *Zoonomia; or the Laws of Organic Life* (Cambridge University Press, 2010).

5   Autobiography, op. cit., p. 80.

6   Autobiography, op. cit., p. 80; Darwin, Francis (ed.), *Life and Letters of Charles Darwin*, Vol. 1, (John Murray, 1887), p. 12.

7   *Life and Letters*, ibid., Vol. 1, p. 11.

8   Ibid., p. 10.

9   Quoted in Browne, Janet, *Charles Darwin: Voyaging* (Jonathan Cape, 1995), p. 19.

10 Autobiography, op. cit., p. 75.

11 Ibid., p. 79.

12 Ibid., p. 91.

13 Ibid., p. 77.

14 CCD Vol. 1, p. 2. *The Correspondence of Charles Darwin* (CCD) stands currently at twenty-one volumes and is being compiled by a team of scholars, working in association with the Cambridge University Press. When complete the Darwin Correspondence Project will run to thirty volumes.

15 Ibid., Vol. 1, p. 1.

16 Ibid., Vol. 1, p. 4.

17 Ibid.

18   Ibid., Vol. 1, p. 121.
19   Ibid., Vol. 1, p. 18.
20   Ibid., Vol. 1, p. 20.
21   Ibid.
22   Autobiography, op. cit., p. 93; *Life and Letters*, op. cit.,
      Vol. 1, p. 36.
23   CCD Vol. 1, p. 27.
24   Ibid., Vol. 1, p. 37.
25   Ibid., Vol. 1, p. 25.
26   Autobiography, op. cit., p. 93.
27   Ibid., p. 100.
28   Ibid.
29   CCD Vol. 1, p. 36.
30   Autobiography, op. cit., p. 102.
31   Ibid., p. 104; *Life and Letters*, op. cit., Vol. 1, p. 52.
32   Autobiography, ibid., p. 108; *Life and Letters*, ibid., Vol. 1, p.
      57.
33   CCD Vol. 1, p. 128.
34   Ibid., Vol. 1, p. 129.
35   Ibid., Vol. 1, p. 132.
36   Ibid., Vol. 1, p. 134.
37   Ibid., Vol. 1, p. 132.
38   Ibid., Vol. 1,p. 141.
39   Ibid., Vol. 1, p. 142.
40   Ibid., Vol. 1, p. 150.
41   Keynes, R.D. (ed.), *Charles Darwin's Beagle Diary*
      (Cambridge University Press, 1988), p. 18.
42   Ibid., p. 21.
43   Ibid., p. 41.
44   Ibid., p. 42.
45   CCD Vol. 1, p. 237.
46   *Origin of Species*, op. cit., p. 65.
47   CCD Vol. 1, p. 236.
48   Ibid., Vol. 1, p. 504.
49   Ibid., Vol. 2, p. 29.
50   Ibid.

51 Autobiography, op. cit., p. 116.
52 CCD Vol. 1, p. 490.
53 Ibid., Vol. 1, p. 503.
54 Ibid., Vol. 1, p. 503.
55 Ibid., Vol. 1, p. 512.
56 Ibid., Vol. 2, p. 91.
57 Ibid., Vol. 2, p. 199.
58 Autobiography, op. cit., p. 142.
59 *Origin of Species*, op. cit., p. 102.
60 Autobiography, op. cit., p. 126.
61 CCD Vol. 1, p. 510.
62 Ibid., Vol. 2, p. 51.
63 Ibid., Vol. 2, p. 444.
64 Healey, Edna, *Emma Darwin: the Inspirational Wife of a Genius* (Hodder Headline, 2001), p. 148.
65 CCD Vol. 2, p. 279.
66 Ibid., Vol. 2, p. 335.
67 Ibid., Vol. 2, p. 172.
68 Darwin, Charles, 'The Foundations of the Origin of Species', in *The Works of Charles Darwin*, Vol. 10 (Pickering & Chatto, 1986), p. xxi.
69 CCD Vol. 3, p. 2.
70 Ibid., Vol. 3, p. 7.
71 Ibid., Vol. 3, p. 10.
72 Ibid., Vol. 5, p. 542.
73 Ibid., Vol. 7, p. 84.
74 Ibid., Vol. 6, p. 89.
75 Ibid., Vol. 6, p. 100.
76 Ibid., Vol. 6, p. 109.
77 Ibid., Vol. 6, p. 107.
78 Ibid., Vol. 7, p. 517.
79 Ibid., Vol. 7, p. 107.
80 Ibid.
81 Ibid., Vol. 7, p. 119.
82 Ibid., Vol. 7, p. 117.
83 Ibid., Vol. 6, p. 387.

84   Browne, J., *Charles Darwin: the Power of Place* (Pimlico, 2003), p. 42.
85   CCD Vol. 7, p. 121.
86   Ibid., Vol. 7, p. 279.
87   Ibid., Vol. 7, p. 298.
88   Ibid., Vol. 7, p. 278.
89   Ibid., Vol. 7, p. 303.
90   Ibid., Vol. 7, p. 298.
91   Ibid., Vol. 7, p. 308.
92   Ibid., Vol. 7, p. 319.
93   Ibid., Vol. 7, p. 278.
94   Ibid., Vol. 7, p. 284.
95   *Origin of Species*, op. cit., p. 459.
96   Ibid., p. 82.
97   Ibid., p. 83.
98   CCD Vol. 7, p. 367.
99   Ibid., Vol. 7, p. 362.
100 Ibid., Vol. 7, p. 371.
101 Ibid., Vol. 6, p. 391.
102 Ibid., Vol. 6, p. 396.
103 *Power of Place*, op. cit., p. 122.
104 CCD Vol. 8, p. 280.
105 Autobiography, op. cit., p. 154.
106 CCD Vol. 8, p. 308.
107 CCD entry 6684, CD to Alfred Russel Wallace, 27 Mar 1869.
108 Darwin, Charles, *The Descent of Man* (Penguin, 2004), p. 689.
109 Ibid., p. 120.
110 Ibid., p. 123.
111 Ibid., p. 120.
112 Ibid., p. 86.
113 Ibid., p. 203.
114 Darwin, Charles, 'The Formation of Vegetable Mould Through the Action of Worms with Observations on their Habits', in *The Works of Charles Darwin*, Vol. 28 (Pickering & Chatto, 1989).
115 Ibid., p. viii.

Timeline

1809	12 February: born in Shrewsbury
1817	Mother, Susannah Wedgwood, dies
1818	Sent to board at Shrewsbury School
1825	Begins medical studies at Edinburgh University; meets Robert Grant
1828	Transfers to Cambridge University and trains for the Church; meets John Henslow
1831	Graduates from Cambridge 27 December: sets sail on HMS *Beagle* on scientific and map-making world voyage
1836	2 October: HMS *Beagle* arrives home in Falmouth Returns to London and is welcomed into scientific society
1839	Publishes his account of his research during the *Beagle* voyage; marries his cousin, Emma Wedgwood; moves to London; first child, William, is born
1841	Second child, Annie, is born
1842	Moves to the village of Downe, Kent, 15 miles south of central London; third child, Mary, is born but dies after three weeks

1843	Starts friendship with Joseph Hooker
1844	Writes unpublished account of his theory of evolution
1846	Research based on *Beagle* collections finally completed
	Begins eight-year project researching classification of the barnacles
1851	Annie, Darwin's eldest daughter, dies
1853	Starts friendship with Thomas Huxley
1855	Starts to write, for publication, a full account of his ideas on evolution
1856	Birth of tenth and last child, Charles Waring
1858	28 June: Charles Waring Darwin dies
	1 July: Lyell and Hooker announce at Linnaean Society the 'Darwin-Wallace theory'
1859	Publication of *The Origin of Species*
1860	Huxley and the Bishop of Oxford debate Darwin's theory
1862	Publication of *On the Various Contrivances by which British and Foreign Orchids are Fertilised by Insects*
1864	Darwin's illness slows all work
1868	Publication of *The Variation of Animals and Plants Under Domestication*
1871	Publication of *The Descent of Man*
1882	19 April: Charles Darwin dies and is buried in Westminster Abbey on 26 April

Further Reading

Browne, Janet, *Charles Darwin: Voyaging* (Jonathan Cape, 1995)

Browne, Janet, *Charles Darwin: The Power of Place* (Jonathan Cape, 2002)

Darwin, Charles, *On the Origin of Species* (Oxford University Press, 2008; first published, 1859)

Darwin, Charles, *The Descent of Man* (Penguin, 2004; first published, 1871)

Dawkins, Richard, *The Blind Watchmaker* (Penguin, 1988)

Desmond, Adrian & Moore, James, *Darwin* (Penguin, 1991)

Desmond, Adrian & Moore, James, *Darwin's Sacred Cause: Race, Slavery and the Quest for Human Origins* (Allen Lane, 2009)

Healey, Edna, *Emma Darwin: the Inspirational Wife of a Genius* (Hodder Headline, 2001)

Gould, Stephen Jay, *Ever Since Darwin* (Norton, 1979)

Gould, Stephen Jay, *The Mismeasure of Man* (Norton, 1996)

Jones, Steve, *Darwin's Island: the Galapagos in the Garden of England* (Little, Brown & Co., 2009)

Keynes, R.D. (ed.), *Charles Darwin's Beagle Diary* (Cambridge University Press, 1988; first published, 1839)

Keynes, Randal, *Annie's Box: Charles Darwin, his Daughter and Human Evolution* (Fourth Estate, 2001)

Milner, Richard, *Darwin's Universe: Evolution from A–Z* (University of California, 2009)

Wallace, Alfred Russel, *The Malay Archipelago* (Oxford University Press, 1986; first published, 1869)

Web Links

www.darwinproject.ac.uk – The letters of Charles Darwin

www.english-heritage.org.uk/daysout/properties/home-of-charles-darwin-down-house – Information from English Heritage about Darwin's home

www.nhm.ac.uk/nature-online/science-of-natural-history/biographies/charles-darwin – Darwin pages curated by London's Natural History Museum

www.wellcome.ac.uk/Funding/Public-engagement/Funded-projects/Major-initiatives/Darwin-200/index.htm – Darwin pages curated by the UK medical charity The Wellcome Trust

www.thebeaglevoyage.com – Darwin's diary of the *Beagle* voyage, presented as a blog

wallaceletters.info – The letters of Alfred Russel Wallace

www.newscientist.com/topic/evolution – New developments and reliable background information on evolutionary theory

www.nature.com/news/specials/darwin – Special edition on evolution from a prestigious science journal

humanorigins.si.edu/resources/intro-human-evolution – The Smithsonian Institution's pages on evolution

Giuseppe Verdi Henry V **Brunel** Pope John Paul II **Jane Austen** William the Conqueror **Abraham Lincoln** Robert the Bruce **Charles Darwin** Buddha **Elizabeth I** Horatio Nelson **Wellington** Hannibal & Scipio **Jesus** Joan of Arc **Anne Frank** Alfred the Great **King Arthur** Henry Ford **Nelson Mandela**